Ian McHarg
Conversations with Students

Conversations with Students,
a Princeton Architectural Press series

Other books in this series

Santiago Calatrava
1-56898-325-5

Le Corbusier
1-56898-196-1

Louis I. Kahn
1-56898-149-x

Rem Koolhaas
1-885232-02-0

Peter Smithson
1-56898-461-8

# Ian McHarg
# Conversations with Students

Dwelling in Nature

Lynn Margulis, James Corner, and Brian Hawthorne, editors
Princeton Architectural Press, New York

Published by
Princeton Architectural Press
37 East Seventh Street
New York, New York 10003

For a free catalog of books, call 1.800.722.6657.
Visit our web site at www.papress.com.

The original audio version of Ian McHarg's "Collaboraton with Nature," an ecological
planning lecture, called "The Lost Tapes of Ian McHarg (2006) (ISBN 1-933392-30-4, 978-
1-933342-30-1) is available on compact disc from Chelsea Green Publishing Company, White
River Junction, Vermont (www.chelseagreen.com).

Project editor: Jennifer N. Thompson
Copyeditor: Scott Tennent
Designer: Jeffrey Lai

Special thanks to: Nettie Aljian, Sara Bader, Dorothy Ball, Nicola Bednarek, Janet
Behning, Becca Casbon, Penny (Yuen Pik) Chu, Russell Fernandez, Wendy Fuller, Sara Hart,
Clare Jacobson, Mark Lamster, Nancy Eklund Later, Linda Lee, Katharine Myers, Lauren
Nelson Packard, Paul Wagner, Joseph Weston, and Deb Wood of Princeton Architectural
Press —Kevin C. Lippert, publisher

Library of Congress Cataloging-in-Publication Data

McHarg, Ian L.

Ian McHarg : conversations with students : dwelling in nature / Lynn Margulis, Brian
Hawthorne, and James Corner, editors.—1st ed.
p. cm.— (Conversations with students)
Includes index.
ISBN-13: 978-1-56898-620-3 (pbk. : alk. paper)
1. Land use—Planning—Environmental aspects. 2. Human ecology. 3. Ecological landscape
design. 4. Landscape architecture—Environmental aspects. I. Margulis, Lynn, 1938-
II. Corner, James, 1961- III. Hawthorne, Brian, 1963- IV. Title.

HD108.6.M39 2006
712—dc22

2006024385

# Table of Contents

Winter in the young forest of rural western Massachusetts.

# Foreword

Alan Berger

Ecological thinking pervades the design world today more than ever. With this book, another generation of landscape architects, architects, and planners, in search of ecological meaning for their work, will find the clarity of Ian McHarg's "conversations" a timely reawakening. McHarg's teaching resisted the "economic" paradigm in lieu of a higher order that could be achieved for our built-natural environment. His ideas challenge the incredible robustness and unrelenting political pressures that threaten collective, long-term, incremental and sustainable planning. McHarg's work reminds us that the greatest plans embody longevity, as evidenced by the man himself. Ian was a tireless advocate for ecological planning. Upon his promotion to Professor Emeritus I asked Ian what his plans were for the upcoming year, to which he replied, "to finish mapping the Earth."[1]

Within these brief essays and recordings one will find the foundations for today's most important systemic landscape thinking used by design professionals: geographic information technology, comprehensive suitability analysis, conservation and performance-based land use planning, thermodynamics and design, to name just a few. Ian crossed over the imaginary lines of landscape architecture, planning, science, anthropology, art, and ethics. Born out of life and death experiences, McHarg cut through the skins separating the academics and architects, whatever their disciplines. He would even find reprehensible the notion of practicing "layer-cake" regional planning without adaptation to the dynamic conditions of contemporary life, cross-disciplinary work, new technologies, social inequity, globalization, and human differences. The lecture published herein, along with the remarkable companion audio recordings, should together be consumed as his "delicious" ninth, tenth, or perhaps eleventh layers of a process that should be left to evolve through disciplinary reorganization and advancement, as if to never receive a final coating of icing.

So how does McHarg's model for ecological planning evolve? Even the great projects based on McHargian theory–the Woodlands of the world–have been encroached by short-term, quick-gain market forces and mentalities. Facing off against, or perhaps slowing down these forces is not what Ian had in mind when he spoke of putting "together again the entire system." He was, instead, brilliantly laying out the next great project for landscape architects: to pick up the pieces of regional systems left in the wake of economic schema, political indecision, ad hoc development, a negligent public and flawed environmental health policy. Our challenge, if we are to build something greater out of the detritus that escaped McHarg's grasp, is to intelligently interpret the systemic thinking brought forth by him to generations of landscape architects and regional planners during the late twentieth century. His model must be implemented both to protect pre-development land, and post-development waste.

To those who never experienced Ian's profound lectures, teachings, or writings, this book serves to begin a conversation that challenges conventional knowledge. Enjoy your journey into the origins of ecological planning.

Notes

1 McHarg's unabridged lecture (pp. 21–74) is available now on audio CD from Chelsea Green Publishing Company. The sound tracks that correspond to the pages in this book are listed below.

**The Lost Tapes of Ian McHarg** CD, 71.33 minutes

# Preface
David Orr

## The "quasi, pseudo, crypto" scientist

Ian McHarg, the booming voice, was in full-stride in the late 1960s. Listen now: let him tell you that he was only a "quasi-pseudo-crypto-scientist" with a no-status theory.[1] Just ignore his loud protest that he was not a scientist; he was more of a scientist than many whom he employed. He was a perceptive observer of the wayward ways of men and their tendency toward selfish destruction of the environment and solipsism. His far-ranging observations and broad descriptions were remarkably accurate. Although not a laboratory or experimental scientist, his commitment to truth, his keen recording skills, and his capacity for communication lead me to claim as vociferously as he denied it: McHarg indeed was a scientist.

In the late 1960s, a time full of controversy, danger, violence, and excitement, I was McHarg's student at the University of Pennsylvania. As the environment became a national issue—even to President Nixon—McHarg was drawn into the eye of the storm. *Design with Nature*, published in 1969, hit public awareness as a bolt of lightning on a dark night. Its second chapter, "The Plight," is one of the finest environmental polemics ever written. And though he was a master of that art, McHarg's point transcended castigation. In proposing a marriage of ecology with landscape architecture, McHarg picked up where Frederick Law Olmsted left off. His aim was to discipline human purposes and growth through a thorough understanding of natural processes. It is a lesson we still struggle to learn.

Although not a student in his department of landscape architecture, I read *Design with Nature* when it first appeared and then sneaked into McHarg's classes at every opportunity. His forthright energy, vision, clarity, and hopefulness were an antidote to the widespread anger and despair of the time. Under his tutelage, landscape architecture, far more than academic theory, was becoming a discipline for the transformation of society. Driven by passion, McHarg developed his litany, his method that later became the basis for Geographic Information Systems (GIS);[2] he developed the concept of requests for "environmental impact statements" to appropriately assign responsibility of environmental degradation. He advocated with clear direction the course toward health of both individuals and, even more so, of communities. A talk by Ian McHarg, full of ribald humor and trenchant perspective, summoned us to act with ecologically informed intelligence toward nature (see footnote, page 8). He helped orient the interests of my lifetime when I was a second-year graduate student.

After graduate school, in 1973, with a colleague I invited McHarg to the Atlanta Environmental Symposium that I had organized. He spoke on the ecological limits to human expansion and kept a large crowd spellbound for an hour and a half. But no amount of good sense about nature and proper land-use sprawl could prevent Atlanta from becoming the sprawl-in-process. Six years later McHarg helped to shape plans for the 1,500 acre non-profit educational center in the Ozarks, that I co-founded. Even at this sub-regional scale his eye picked out details and context with great clarity.

McHarg was a chain smoker and non-stop talker, but on his Ozark sojourn there was a moment in which he stopped both. He asked me to take him to the top of a ridge six hundred feet above the valley floor, to see the lay of the land. Given the state of our equipment and the roads at the time the best way to get there, other than by an arduous hike, was in a model "A" outfitted with twelve forward speeds, a vehicle that could nearly climb a tree. The logging road flaunted two perilous switchbacks and narrowed to the width of a cow path. On our left as we approached the first switchback the ground fell away to a sheer cliff several hundred feet above the hollow. Ian was uneasy, but continued to smoke and talk—until he saw that the path we headed for angled up to forty degrees or so toward the first switchback, where he uttered a fervent "Oh my God" in his pronounced Scottish brogue. Aiming to free both hands for the impending emergency, he absently took the gas cap for an ash tray. He reached through the empty windshield frame to stamp out his cigarette. I meant to blurt out *"don't do that!"* but, as if in a bad dream's stuck-in-molasses action, my words just would not come. Ashes mingled with gas sloshing around in the cap. But God must have heard my silent invocation: nothing exploded. Red-faced, he held on to the windshield frame. Tenacious to a degree limited only to Scots in desperate straits, he remained silent as I slowly backed us up to the second switchback and then proceeded forward to the top of the ridge. His face lightened, a shade paler than I'd recalled just minutes before. He became rather more humble, a remarkable thing in itself. After he surveyed the lay of the land, he confessed the need for "a wee bit of exercise." Rather than return to the 12 speed vehicle, he hiked down the precipice.

My last formal interaction with McHarg was in a course we co-taught as visiting lecturers at Ball State University in Kentucky in 1995. He no longer taught at Penn, nor was he affiliated with his firm Wallace, McHarg, Roberts, and Todd. Still irrepressible, irreverent, and full of good ecological sense, we had a fine time together. In his last decade he took on other, smaller opportunities, and continued gamely, as he mentioned in his autobiography, to "maintain dignity, act with generosity and perhaps with wisdom, continue to seek and solve problems, recover from assault and insult."[3]

McHarg's legacy as a theoretician, organizer, teacher, writer, speaker, and environmentalist transcends any personal reminiscence. He prepared several generations of students to be wise, competent, and imaginative practitioners. A provocative thinker and superb communicator, he inspired a reading and listening public. His contributions to our understanding of how we humans might struggle less and fit more harmoniously with nature are prodigious. McHarg's stature notwithstanding, designing with nature is still the exception. Why? McHarg with other great figures of the mid-twentieth century, including Rachel Carson and Aldo Leopold, were correct; but they and their heirs labored against a tide: that Man must dominate Nature. Technology, population growth, economic expansion, and especially the exuberance of inexpensive fossil fuel powered culture. Leopold's land ethic opposed prevalent and pervasive capitalism, the belief, as articulated by Katharine Hepburn in the classic film, "African Queen," that "Nature is what God put us on Earth to rise above." The opposition to Carson's *Silent Spring*, orchestrated by the chemical industry, rooted in mindless technological optimism, was willful denial.

The reaction to McHarg, both theoretician and practitioner, was more complicated. He took pains to show that designing with, not against, the ecological grain was advantageous to everyone. After unsuccessful polemics McHarg turned to the language of practical self-interest joined by long-term sustainability. Why was his appeal ignored? Why does it continue to fall on deaf ears?

A reason cited by McHarg was the hold of reductionism on the academic curriculum of its graduates.[4] We still educate and investigate in those hermetically sealed boxes we call disciplines. The academy trains specialists— experts exempted from the perception of patterns, even punished when they stray beyond their discipline to comprehend systems. Another reason for the systemic ignorance of McHarg's vision stems, I think, from our ambiguous feelings toward land. Although we celebrate the fecundity and beauty of North America, we perceive it as a marketable commodity. Real estate, a means to personal riches, no one comprehends as a living entity. From the beginning of the so-called New World , cheap land for speculation, mining, forestry, farming–extractive uses–was the original appeal. All along, the ideal has been to defend the freedom to do as one pleases, to pollute with impunity: vandalism, amplified by exploits of global corporations, cooperative legislation and enabling legal practice thinly disguised by the rhetoric of the market. Indeed, McHarg's words have lasting value:

> We have but one explicit model of the world and that is built upon economics....Money is our measure, convenience is its cohort, the short term is its span, and the devil may take the hindmost is the morality.... Neither love nor compassion, health nor beauty, dignity nor freedom, grace nor delight are important unless they can be priced....[5]

Finally, a third reason for the resistance to McHarg's admonition to design with nature is the feebleness of the political system when confronted with systemic problems. We might have charted a different direction: between 1968 and 1980, Republicans and Democrats worked together to lay the foundation for a national environmental policy that included the National Environmental Policy Act, the Clean Air Act, the Clean Water Act, and the Endangered Species Act. But, by rejection of the idea of a national land-use policy–a portent of worse to come–they stumbled in 1974. For a quarter of a century, the cause of ecological enlightenment and decent land use has languished. McHarg's idea of rational and healthy land use, of dwelling in nature, is anathema to the political spectrum that calls itself "conservative." Each year they find less to conserve–in fact, less even to exploit other than rules of the game by which a few are greatly enriched. Ignorant of the photoautotrophic and chemoautotrophic sources of energy, they believe, to their own detriment, that the world was made for man as the only superior form of life.

McHarg's vision of humankind and nature in harmony, here in this book, in his own voice, may help generate wisdom and foresight amongst your peers. We bring to you these conversations in his inimitable voice, and you will immediately see that his advice and enlightened view retains incontrovertible relevance to our social lives today. I admire and want to share with you the optimism, the active ingenuity, and most of all the transcendent teaching I found so intrinsic to the legacy of Ian McHarg.

Notes
1  See "The Theory of Creative Fitting," in this volume, 21.
2  Ibid., 21.
3  Ian McHarg, *A Quest for Life: An Autobiography* (New York: Wiley, 1996), 334.
4  Ian McHarg and Frederick R. Steiner, *To Heal the Earth: Selected Writings of Ian L. McHarg* (Washington, DC: Island Press, 1998).
5  Ian McHarg, *Design with Nature* (New York: Wiley, 1969), 25.

# Acknowledgments
Lynn Margulis

"What modern science is...the egg is shattered...fragments lie scattered on the ground."

We applaud the foresight of our Boston University colleague James G. Schaadt, whose enthusiasm for McHarg's ideas and common sense led him in 1976 to preserve on tape the collection of McHarg's lectures entitled *Collaboration with Nature.* Many thanks to Lorraine Olendzenski, who with Jim and me worked for many years to make these scientific lecture tapes— by eminent scientists from Harvard, MIT, and elsewhere–available. All of them deal with the effect of life on planet Earth. We also thank Adam MacConnell, superb Master's degree candidate in geosciences, who tediously spliced and copied for months in order to recover and compile all of the segments recorded on McHarg's eight different cassettes. Adam recovered ninety-nine percent of McHarg's Scottish-accented lecture on a single cassette. We are grateful to James MacAllister, an accomplished videographer, who then ran the audiosignal through a graphic equalizer and applied a digital noise filter to restore McHarg's natural tones. Our fine editor, Brian Hawthorne, transformed the oral into the written word. He digitized, transcribed, and edited McHarg's clear vision. The recording made such an impression on Brian that he was inspired to spend countless unpaid hours learning about McHarg's field of landscape architecture at the junction of environmental science and planning. We are extremely grateful to Leslie Sauer (former McHarg secretary) for her enthusiastic last minute provision of McHarg's unpublished poem and to our scientific associate, Dr. Michael Chapman, who, with his usual diligence and insight, contributed late-stage editorial corrections and revisions to the manuscript. We are grateful to Paul Frederick Steiner, Dean of the School of Architecture at the University of Texas and editor of *Ecological Design and Planning* (Wiley, 1996) for access to his extensive work on McHarg's bibliography and curriculum vitae. Steiner's list was essential to the production of our manuscript. We also thank Margo Baldwin, Chelsea Green Publishing Company, who enthusiastically agreed to publish the CD of McHarg's booming voice in his lecture and audience questions. (To purchase the CD see www.chelseagreen.com).

We direct the interested reader to two books that may provide clues to why we tend to destroy the planetary surface that sustains us. I suspect McHarg would have liked them had he lived: Reg Morrisons's *A Spirit in the Gene: Humanity's Proud Illusion and the Laws of Nature* (Cornell University Press, 1999), and John Skoyles and Dorion Sagan's *Up from Dragons: On the Evolution of Human Intelligence* (McGraw Hill, 2002). From the latter we see that the greatest hypertrophy in the chimp-human transition was the proliferation of frontal cortex neurons dedicated to our social lives. We are so concerned with what our associates think and say about us that careful and quantitative planning is alien. Our faculties for exactitude, measurement, and logical estimate are wantonly abandoned by each of us when aroused by sexual opportunity. Especially the adult male *Homo sapiens*, Morrison reminds us, will delude himself to behave as if he were invincible in any perceived incursion on his sexual prerogatives. The rational activity of ecological planning, the imperative to nurture and heal the land, the slow frustration of joint and co-operative decision-making so necessary for large-scale collaboration with nature, is at odds with our impulses. Even the explicit and honest assessment of the client's "needs and desires," the straightforward, clear statement of the underlying value system required to convert a meadow to a shopping mall or a wetland to a university campus evokes a dilemma.

Our last and greatest praise is reserved for McHarg himself, who, after Frederick Law Olmsted, is arguably the most influential landscape architect this country has ever seen. Consider the immediate relevance, indeed the urgency, of his now thirty-year-old message. McHarg's appeal to logic and foresight, to analysis and prediction of the consequences of ignoring the past history of the landscape, and his dedication to the common good should certainly appeal to reason. Yet our rational mindset falls victim to the emotional impatience by which it is inevitably eclipsed.

Will our rapacious "civilization" ever be ready to heed McHarg's notice that we imperil ourselves, that we ourselves are "the most endangered species?" Will we ever mature to a point where we can cherish the bedrock, the mountains, the forest, the fields and seas that sustain us? In our mad rush to "progress," to ownership of the landscape, will we pause mindfully to plan? I suspect we will not. I have a hunch we can not behave so contrarily to our nature. But I fervently hope I am mistaken. I hope that like McHarg we will be brave in our decisions and open to the luxuriant influx of scientific truth, of measurements we do not necessarily like, and observations that do not necessarily support our cherished beliefs. I hope we will respect hard-acquired fact. McHarg's love of the land, his willingness to watch, to listen, and to act with alacrity and to brave the gossip and the mediocrity, eschew nonsense in even the highest places, make his inspirational words so relevant to our actions today.

# The Theory of Creative Fitting

Ian L. McHarg

"I am not a scientist"

A McHarg news clipping, "Ian McHarg, 29, married, became a father during a week's postponement of his thesis. From Glasgow, he served seven years in the British Army and was a Major of parachute troops. Up all night, he fell asleep in the bathtub before his thesis jury met."

I would first like to establish that I am not a scientist. However, I think that all the ecology I have ever learned I learned from good scientists. From them I have developed a theory—one which has absolutely no status whatsoever, except insofar as all the parts have been derived from excellent scientists.

I once gave a lecture on this theory to Brookhaven National Laboratory. At the end, the president of that lab said that mine was a most astonishing theory—astonishing, he said, because the theory had come from a landscape architect! Nonetheless, it was sufficiently good that it deserved the attention of better men. As someone who might be called a "crypto-pseudo-quasi-scientist," this was, I think, the best encomium I have ever enjoyed.

The theory has four elements. The first recognizes something called creativity, which can be defined as the employment of energy and matter to raise matter and energy to higher levels of order. This then has an antithesis, which is reduction: the movement from higher to lower levels of order. One can envisage it very simply, by thinking about a forest, with all the plants and animals and microorganisms within it. Imagine now that all the fanciest scientists in the world inventory all of the components of this elaborate forest ecosystem and, after having done so, burn it. According to the first law of thermodynamics, no matter will have been created nor destroyed. Nevertheless, the matter assuredly will have gone from a higher to a lower level of order. Creativity is the antithesis of this. Starting from a primeval universe, the evolution of the elements in the periodic table—hydrogen, helium, lithium beryllium—would correspond to my definition of creativity. The employment of energy and matter to raise matter and energy to a higher level of order occurred in the origin of the heavier elements. The evolution of the phylogenetic scale of plants and animals also corresponds exactly to my thermodynamic concept of creativity. Evolution, then, can be subsumed within this term of creativity. Evolution, both physical and biological, has been creative.

The next element of the theory is the existence of criteria by which we can identify directionality and attributes of the creative process. Creativity, according to this definition, always shows the tendency to move from a greater to a lesser randomness, from simplicity to complexity, from uniformity to diversity, from instability toward dynamic equilibrium, from a low to a high number of species, from a low to a higher number of symbioses. These tendencies can be subsumed under two terms: in the left-hand column, the tendency toward entropy, or disorder; on the positive side of the balance sheet, the tendency toward negentropy, or a higher level of order. The theory allows us to see the state of any process and its directionality. Is the process creative and evolving, or is it retrogressing? If we can see the directionality we have a very useful model. If one sees anything that goes from complexity to simplicity, presumably it is reductive and retrogressing. If we see a process move from instability to stability or to dynamic equilibrium, presumably it is evolving and creative.

It would be very useful if there were some sort of criterion that allowed us to look at any process and decide whether or not it was creative. I think there is such a criterion; it is described by the verb *to fit*, which derives two meanings from two different people, Sir Charles Darwin and Lawrence Henderson. Darwin simply said, among other things, that the surviving organism is fit for the environment. Henderson said that the actual environment, the actual world, constitutes the fittest possible

Charles Darwin and Lawrence Henderson

abode for life–for every form of life that has existed, does now exist, and all imaginable forms that can exist. I think one can take these two propositions, unite them, and also make them dynamic. One can say that there is a requirement for any system–whether it is sub-cellular, cell, tissue, organism, individual, family, institution–to find the most fit of all environments, and to adapt both that environment and the system itself. The environment and the system must fit. This fitting then is essential to survival, according to Darwin, and there is always a most fit environment for every system seeking an environment.

The next most important point in my theory is to define creativity. The ability to find of all environments the most fit, and to adapt that environment and oneself, is in fact a creative process. Again, according to Darwin, if there are two species (and species, by definition, differ) both in exactly the same environment—the same impingement of radiation, the same availability of nutrients, the same habitat opportunities in the system—one of these species will triumph. One of them will survive; the other will become extinct. Survival is contingent on the surviving organism accomplishing the least-work, maximum-benefit solution. It is thermodynamically creative. The surviving species is better able to select from all environmental choices that most fit environment. The surviving species creatively adapts itself, and better adapts the environment to accomplish this fitting. Therefore creativity is not some attribute of painters and sculptors alone; it is not an attribute of only a very select part of society. My model suggests rather that creativity has permeated the evolution of matter and life, and actually is indispensable for the survival of any system.

Now, what do we need for analyses? We would like to have a synoptic attribute, which would allow us, at any point in time, to determine whether any system in fact accomplishes creative fitting. I believe that such an attribute is the presence of health. One has to be careful how one uses the term "health." There are two definitions that I like best. The first is that health is the capability of recovery from insult; this is an adaptive criterion. Second, the World Health Organization defines a healthy man as one who not only solves problems but also seeks them. That corresponds very well with this definition of creative fitting, whereby any system is required to find of all environments the most fit, to adapt that environment, and to adapt itself.

So, that is the theory. It is simple minded, but then I am simple minded. I am not a scientist. It has to be simple, or I would not have discovered it. It has to be simple, or I would not be able to use it. That is it. There is something called creativity. We can identify creative fitting. Creative fitting is absolutely required for any system, be it a social system or a natural system. The accomplishment of creative fitting will be revealed in health. I recognize, in fact, a single phenomenon that we call "creative fitting in health," and its antithesis, called "reductive misfit revealed in pathology." Any physical, social, or mental pathology in a human or physiological non-human system gives us incontrovertible evidence that the system is temporarily or permanently unable to find, of all environments, the most fit, and/or to adapt itself to that environment. The extension \of this pathology, of course, will be morbidity–whether of cell, tissue, organ, organism, species, ecosystem, or social system. Wherever you find evidence of health–the capability to recover from insult, or the capacity to not only solve problems but to seek them–you have, I would suggest, incontrovertible evidence that the system has been able to identify the most fit environment, to adapt that environment, and to adapt itself. This is creative fitting revealed in health.

# Definition of the Natural Environment
"I have developed a litany"

This is the model I use as a teacher and as a practitioner in ecological planning. I take money from people for services. I take
money to help them in the course of creative fitting, whether
it be a group of people who wish to build a new town, or to
develop a metropolitan plan for a region, or simply to develop
very small tracts of housing. My role in every case is to find,
of all environments the most fit, and to adapt that environment.
I help the consumer adapt the environment and themselves to
accomplish creative fitting.

How do we go about this? First, one has to define the region
in which one works. In most cases, this is defined by the client.
The definition of the region is of course impossible, because the
Earth is finally not divisible, so I say the region is defined by the
area within which the creative fitting must occur. The accomplishment of the fitting will be revealed in the health of the
consumer. So we define the region, and then we have to define
the environment, because of our engagement in two things. The
environment, again according to Henderson, has every opportunity that the consumer needs. We have to define the consumer's
needs and desires and we have to identify the ability of the
environment to satisfy these. The situation is dynamic: to
accomplish creative fitting involves modification of both the
consumer and the environment.

After defining the region, the question is to identify those scientists who can describe the environment. Because I am simple

minded, and I like to go on a simple progression, I have developed a litany. The litany involves a number of scientists who I hire, coerce, and induce to describe the region, because of course at first I know nothing about any region. I will not open my mouth to say anything until I am advised by those people who do know it. I always begin with a bedrock geologist, because in many of the parts of the world where I live and work the geology reveals a billion years of evidence. A billion years is a lot of evidence, and I want to start with the oldest, best, longest evidence. I ask the bedrock geologist to simply identify the region in terms of geological phenomena, which he knows how to do beautifully. All geologists know how to define the region and they are always gratified to have the opportunity to do so. As I pay them for their services, they have even more reason to be gratified! Next, I always find a meteorologist, preferably a biometeorologist. I ask him to identify the region in question by following the phenomena of climate. The meteorologist sets off very merrily, and he identifies every single piece of information about the climate of the region. Following the meteorologist, I seek a geomorphologist. The bedrock geologist needs not necessarily know about the recent events that shape the landscape–the Pleistocene geology. If he does not, we hire a surficial geologist, who identifies kames and kettles, eskers and glacial landforms–all those lovely expressions of glacial history, the last million years or so of the Pleistocene. Once we have that information, we are in a position to hire a groundwater hydrologist. So we hire him, and he identifies the phenomenon of groundwater hydrology. Then we hire a surface water hydrologist and a physical geographer to

explain the physiography. Then we find a soil scientist to identify soils and their variability, and then a plant ecologist and an
animal ecologist. I develop a layer cake. I generally collect the
information about a region in this way because it allows me to
see causality. Each identification of these phenomena I put on a
single map. Then I overlay one on top of another.

This leads us to our second objective. After identification of
the region in terms of phenomena—after we make our layer-cake
map—we want to know about the region in terms of process.
Everything is always changing. Everything is now and has
always been the phenomena, the course of becoming something
else. To understand what it is now, one must go through the
process of finding out what it has been. In Pennsylvania, right
where I live now, there used to be mountains twenty-seven
thousand feet high. Now they are six hundred feet high. The
fact of the matter is the area cannot be understood except in the
context of a great mountain range of the past. Indeed, what we
call mountains fifteen hundred feet high not very far from my
home can only be comprehended as former oceans, remains of
ancient seas. This of course is the part of geology that constitutes an astonishing novelty for most people. Most people have
never studied geology. Yet it is very clear that the understanding
of bedrock and surficial geology is indispensable to the understanding of process.

So again we hire the very same people. We now ask them
to review the material in terms of process. We ask them to tell
us what is now, in terms of what has been. We ask: what are
the dynamics of the process? Here the structure begins to have

some sort of value, because if we start off with bedrock geology, the evolution in the geology, and the evolution in the
climate—pre-Pleistocene and then Pleistocene—the interaction
of climate and bedrock geology allows us to understand surficial geology. Other factors are operating, but clearly these two
are the major ones. Ten thousand feet of ice left a very large
mark. Staten Island, for example, is still rising from the receding
ice. Indicators of the Pleistocene ice age are still with us. The
understanding of the interaction of climate and bedrock geology allows us to see what the geomorphologist studies—the
surficial geology. At this point then, the surficial geology can
be interpreted by the groundwater hydrologist. The hydrologist
does not produce new information; all he does is take information that is given to him by the bedrock and surficial geologists, and he reinterprets these data in terms of groundwater
hydrology. The physiographer comes along. He has seen the
evolution of the physiography in terms of long-term geological
evolution, substantially modified by the Pleistocene. He can
then interpret the current surface in terms of physiography, as
it is only the exposed part of the Pleistocene and the exposed
bedrock geology that we see. The physiographer explains the
surface in terms of slope, hills and valleys, deltas and kames
and kettles and escarpments, and other surface features. At this
point, we can talk to a surface-water hydrologist. A substantial
portion of his interpretation will derive from the information
from the climate interaction on bedrock, surficial geology,
and on groundwater hydrology. This allows him to talk about
surface-water hydrology and the interchange between surface

and groundwater hydrology. Given that, then one is able to talk about soils, because soils are only a byproduct of processes. All of the data that define the processes derive from the interaction of climate on bedrock and surficial geology, groundwater and surface-water hydrology, and physiography. Taken together, these allow us to understand the variability of soils. Having understood the factors that influence the variability of soils, we can begin to understand the variability of plants. A plant ecologist, in identifying the variability in the successional zones of plants, must invoke all the information from climate, geology, geography, physiography, hydrology, and soil. Once we have reached that point, we can then begin to talk about the variability of animals. All animals are related to plants, either in the first or in the second degree. Either animals eat the plants or they eat the animals who eat the plants. The variability of animal habitats can only be described in terms of the variability of plants. But the plants and their variability are related to the variability of climate and soils, and so on and so forth, and back we go.

# Synthesis of an Ecological Model
"Information fragmented is of no use to anybody"

This absolutely delicious process, which of course is an education for me, is paid for by someone else and performed by someone else. At the end of the process, I have some understanding about the region in terms of both phenomena and of process. But process *per se* is not really what interests me. All of these

data gathered from many sources describe one whole system,
only divided by language and by science. Our job is to reconstitute the region and all its processes again, like putting together
Humpty Dumpty.

> Humpty Dumpty sat on a wall,
> Humpty Dumpty had a great fall,
> All the King's horses and all the King's men,
> Couldn't put Humpty together again.

This is what modern science is: the egg is shattered, all the
fragments lie scattered on the ground. The fragments are called
geology and physics and chemistry and hydrology and soil
science, plant ecology, animal ecology, molecular biology, and
political science. There is *no one* who can put together again the
entire system. Information fragmented is of no use to anybody.
What we always need to proceed is really the one whole system,
the entire region in question, so for design of sensible human
land-use somebody has to put it together again.

Science and university departments are devices by which
integration is all but impossible. As we know, academics resist
integration with incredible ferocity. Obviously, one must be
emasculated and myopic in order to be a pure, successful scientist. Because of the requirement scientists in universities have
for purity and success, clearly the integration needed is resisted
by scientists. Holism therefore is extremely difficult. The only
coercive device I have that aids the necessary integration of the
voracious but knowledgeable professionals is called "money."

When I have a client who insists that I interpret the region, the whole system, then of course I have to find scientists who will make the system whole—and I pay them.

And so we set the scientists this very difficult task for which they are remarkably untrained. We ask them to group together all these independent spectral views of the universe into one whole system. It is very difficult, but once one has it, one has the best description natural science can give us of the region that functions as a single interacting process understood in the context of its long past. By this time, we have an ecological model. The model can be one of many sorts. It can be descriptive, or it can be a graphically represented model, like a layer cake, in which transparent maps are systematically overlain on other maps. At the bottom is the oldest process, bedrock geology; the next level is surficial geology; the surficial geology can be interpreted in terms of groundwater and surface water hydrology; if possible, the surficial geology is interpreted in terms of physiography; the physiography is interpreted in terms of soils and their variability; the plants in the soil are seen on top; the animals, including man, are then seen on top of the plants; finally, we have the macroclimate, the mesoclimate, and the microclimate.

This then is the regional "universe." In certain special conditions you may have to include other views—those of physical oceanographers, limnologists, and so on—but by and large, the group of people I spoke about, those that form the eight-layer cake of our model, suffices for most terrestrial conditions.

This approach of course can also be computerized. There are computer scanners that can handle something the size of a state geology map. We can take such a colored map with perhaps a billion bits of information, and we can digitize this into the computer in fewer than ten seconds.

At the end of the layer process we have an ecological model. Not only is it a descriptive model, but it should be a predictive model as well. Because the system is an interactive system, we should be able to say, "If nitrates are dumped into the system here, they should show up as blue baby syndrome there," or, as in the Rocky Mountain National Arsenal in Denver, "If you dump selenium, cyanide, and arsenic into the ground, then it is likely to show up, as it does, in people's drinking water nearby." I call this poison at Federal expense. We should be able to say, "if you affect the system here, there will be repercussions." We should be able to predict something about the location and nature of these repercussions.

# The Phenomena and Processes of the Human Environment
"The masochism that is part of the Scottish character"

This exercise provides us with an ecological model. But, finally, we are not concerned with plants and animals. We do not worry here about plants and animals, because our real concern is man. The only truly endangered species is man. If man is eliminated by atomic holocaust or any other man-made device, I think we can be quite sure that evolution will start again. The algae will laugh. "Next time no brains," they will say, and evolution will proceed into some lovely new expression. We really have to be concerned with man, and we would like to deal with him as rigorously as we have been able to deal with the region through the natural sciences. Perhaps to deal with man is a little bit more difficult, but nonetheless let us proceed.

We try to identify the region in terms of human phenomena and human processes. We try to make a human ecological model. For the phenomena, this is quite easy because the census generally provides all the information we need. We can first identify the population by age, sex, ethnicity, occupation, education, employment or lack of employment, and by type of residence and other factors. We can identify the institutions of commerce, industry, and transportation. We can define and locate spatially all the social phenomena that constitute the region. Having done this, however, we want to see these phenomena in terms of process. You and I and everyone else are inexplicable, except in terms of process. You and I cannot be understood, except in the context of our parents, their parents, and the rest of our histories. There is variability with people; to plan the human landscape one must know their particularities and preferences. The game of ecological planning, of landscape architecture, is to match people's needs and desires to the environmental opportunities.

Let us discuss the matter of social process. To proceed we need to understand the variability of people, their specific needs and desires. Perhaps the best way to approach needs and desires, at least the way I have tended to do so is to employ cultural anthropologists, and to go through an exercise of identifying historical and cultural evolution. We start then with the biophysical field that has been described in the ecological model, and begin with the primeval occupants, the Indians. We identify

McHarg working on his thesis project at Harvard University.

patterns–their circulation patterns, settlement patterns, and land-use patterns–and see the biophysical field, the region adapted by these people to fit.

Then we see the European colonists as they arrive. We identify their sites of emigration, as far as we can, and identify the attitudes they have to each other and to the land. We try to assess the particular adaptive skills they brought with them, and their particular preferences for the environment, which in many cases are related to their adaptive skills: their ability to farm or fish or mine or lumber or engage in commerce. We see readily that these different ethnic groups come from different environments, that they seek environments that correspond to those that they left, and that they seek the opportunity to practice their adaptive skills. Their historic adaptive skills, the adaptations they accomplished on the land, permit us to try to understand as best we can why they chose the environments they chose. One cannot understand the pattern of settlement of Scots in North America, for instance, unless one understands the masochism that is part of the Scottish character, and which is well revealed in their brand of Christianity, Presbyterianism.

The Scots have always had an unerring ability to be able to find thin, poor soils to perpetuate that poverty to which they were so long accustomed. It is no surprise to find that they occupy Labrador or Nova Scotia (New Scotland), eastern Canada or northern Ontario, upstate Pennsylvania, the mountains of North Carolina, or the mountains of Georgia. Here, people who were able to find thin, poor soils and unproductive agriculture, were able to maintain that masochism and poverty for which they were particularly well suited.

The German immigrants, of course, were different. They knew about deep, rich, limestone soils. They knew that the black walnut tree (*Juglans nigra*) was an indicator of these soils. The Amish and Mennonites unerringly were able to find rich, deep, fat, productive soils. And they built fat, productive farms.

So we begin with this exercise of being able to understand people and their proclivities, their attitudes toward the land, their adaptive skills. We see why they selected the environments they selected. We record this–we lay down the settlements and their adaptations by use of a succession of land maps organized by date: 1750, 1800, 1850, 1900, 1910, 1920, 1930, and so forth. Suddenly, at the end of this, we gain an idea of the processes. Through history, and through the eyes of the cultural anthropologist, we begin to see the pattern, and to understand the pattern and distribution of people, land-use, and institutions.

Once we have the historical record, we are confronted with the much more difficult task of making an ecological model. The academic science of ecology in the twentieth century has preoccupied itself mainly with plants and animals. It sees man as a polluter of natural systems. Only a very small effort has expanded to try to make a human ecology. As a result, it is far more difficult for us to make a human ecological model than to make an ecological model of non-human, natural systems.

Of all the attempts to make ecological models, perhaps the most useful is that developed by the epidemiologists. They use a concept described variously as a *community health index* or as a community integration/disintegration index. This is simply a device where certain parameters are selected, including the relative age of the population, gender distribution, income, occupation, the amount of education, certain factors of crime, certain factors of disease, amount of transience, and so on. We try to assemble an index of forty or fifty descriptions of the social institutions.

Let us use a community in which most of the people are elderly—for example Jim Thorpe in Pennsylvania, which is an abandoned deep coal-mining town. Most of the people there are old, and when they die, the place will die. Obviously this is an aberration, a sort of social pathology. One has a norm, one calculates deflection from this norm for each of the categories, and one simply aggregates the values. A value then for the healthiest community in the region under study can be composed with one with the greatest pathology. This effectively allows one to make an ecological model in which the region in terms of social, physical, and mental health can be identified and the community health index measured.

There must be other and better ways. This is not the method most often used now. Generally, the economic model is used. More money is assumed to mean better health. This, of course, is not true. No clear correlation between money and health has been documented. Rather, there are specific diseases of the rich: cirrhosis of the liver, heart disease, and kidney disease. Indeed, the diseases of stress are very much the diseases of wealth. The human ecological model is a much less comprehensive one than those developed by plant and animal ecologists. But it would seem to have the greatest utility as an indicator—a view of the degree of success in adaptation of institutions, families, or groups within a region, which allows one to see a hierarchy from the absolute behavioral sink of human pathology at the bottom to the highest accomplishment of physical, social, and mental health at the top.

This is point one; we then go through stage two. We have been able to see people in context of their historic adaptation to a known biophysical field, which was a social value system to which the people variously responded. The present local inhabitants, their institutions, and their land-use patterns constitute then the sum of all their adaptations—some successful, some neutral, some failures. Their adaptations are reflected in their institutions, in how they invest their capital and their infrastructure: buildings, places, and spaces. We now are able to see the present in terms of the interaction of a people on a biophysical field over time.

## Intrinsic Suitabilities
"We have asked Nature to tell Man what it is"

Next we try to return to the biophysical field and to view the opportunities and constraints it offers both to present consumers and to the future. We engage in the crucially important planning process. We seek to find the most fit of all environments. We want to help consumers, people in general, to find the most fit environment. We want to help them modify that environment and modify themselves to accomplish creative fitting. The field from which one searches for these propitious environments is, of course, the biophysical field described above in the ecological model. However, we must interpret it. We now have to think of our goal not only in terms of an inter-action of biophysical processes but also as a social value system, wherein all the opportunities and constraints afforded by the system are, in fact, represented. This means, then, that we must reconstitute our data in a different form. No longer is it simply geology for the sake of geologists, or hydrology for the sake of hydrologists. The rock, water, and soil become resources for the sake of those who plan to live in the region, the prospective consumers. We must go through every single one of the categories with all of the data that we have identified—all of the data on bedrock geology, climate, surficial geology, groundwater hydrology, limnology, soils, plants, animals, and land-use—in order to reorganize it. We make suitability classes in which all of the factors that are most propitious for each one of the larger land users are identified.

Of course, this exercise can be done at any scale: at the scale of a single person who wants to locate a home, or a group of people who want to locate a communal farm. The exercise, depending on the client, can be operated at the scale of a single landowner who wants to locate a second home, say, with an on-site septic tank and an on-site well. Or the entire process may be scaled far larger, operated for someone like me who looks to locate a new town for 150,000 people. One must be sure that one knows who or what the consumer is, knows the needs and desires of those who will occupy the region. One must have a databank in which the needs and desires of the consumer are actually identified and accurately enumerated.

Let us take something very simple, like agriculture by type. Let us assume our clients are consumers of agricultural land: row crop agriculture, crop agriculture, long-rotation agriculture with a lot of pasture. We will then enumerate the factors of climate and find out which are most propitious for their preferred style of agriculture. We note the total number of frost-free days, the amount of insolation, the amount of precipitation, the actual incidence of winter and summer precipitation, the presence or absence of hurricanes, tornados, or other intense storms. We identify from our databank all of the climate factors that are most propitious for this type of agriculture, and all of the factors that are most detrimental. We record these two groups for climate–detrimental and beneficial–and then do the same for bedrock geology. In agriculture, geology in its raw form is not so terribly important, although there is now in the United States Geological Survey a group that is working on the geochemistry of disease. Alumina in soils was apparently responsible for widespread goiter in West Virginia. That, clearly, is a component of geology, which might also be important in agriculture. However, one goes through each of these categories. Certainly physiography matters very much, because row crop agriculture requires very flat slopes. The slope must be from 0–5%. Soils, clearly, are enormously important to agriculture; the physical texture of soils, the permeability, the seasonal high water table, acidity and alkalinity, are certainly very important. We select the most favorable aspects of soils, of vegetation, and if this were important, of wildlife, and any other factors important to the client.

The search for intrinsic suitabilities is done for any prospective land-use. This description is a mere example of how it might be done for agriculture. The more information we have, the more discriminating we can be. We can assess the soil for agriculture by type, including for special crops like wild rice, or rice and catfish, or cranberries, or whatever is important for the specific area, for the specific needs and desires of the client.

If we can identify what the consumer needs, it should be possible to work with the inventory of information on air, land, water, life, and location, and identify the factors that are most propitious. We also identify all the factors that are detrimental. We then attempt to solve the convergence problem, either with a computer or in a handcrafted way. We identify where all or most of the propitious factors are present, and hopefully where none or few of the detrimental ones are present. In that way we develop a plan that begins with the most suitable location for any prospective land-use.

It is important to recognize that this is a relative system. We seek a realistic solution, one that is the most fit within the region. The most fit within one region may not be anything like the most fit in another. In New England, I suspect, there are no farming opportunities that equal those available in the Great Plains. Nonetheless, there are areas that are most fit within the region. We can do this for agriculture by type, industry by type, recreation by type, urbanization by categories of residence by type, style, size, income, residence by density, or residence by coverage. If we can specify the land-use in terms of air, land, water, life, and location, there will emerge ways by which you can identify the most fit environment.

We can do that for every single land-use. The land-use list allows us to categorize the opportunities for broad groups of consumers. Then we begin to assess values for multiple uses. That is, certain land-uses are compatible and can coexist with others. Pasture agriculture or long-rotation agriculture can coexist with appropriate wildlife management, and with recreation. Other types of residence–second homes for instance–easily coexist with recreation, and many other multiple coexisting functions can be recognized. We could manage one single land area for recreation, for some commercial forestry, for wildlife management, for flood control, for water yield, and so on. It is not only quite possible to identify the region by intrinsic suitability for single uses, but also it is possible to identify ones which happily sustain multiple, constant, complementary, coexisting land uses. Of course, we need also to identify areas in competition, those which are coequally suitable for two uses that are not compatible. The search for lands which are suitable for playing fields or intensive recreation are likely to select land which is coequally suitable for regional shopping centers, for light industry, and so on.

One has to be able to make clear for the region the intrinsic suitabilities for all prospective land-uses. We need to grade from most to least suitable those areas that are intrinsically suitable for compatible, coexisting uses, and recognize those areas that are equally suitable for uses which are, in fact, competitive and antagonistic. When we have done this, we will have already identified the region with the people in the region, who have become the consumers. We have developed an intrinsic social value system in which every part of that system is more or less suitable for every prospective land use. We have made a synthesis of intrinsic suitability. We have asked Nature to tell Man what it is, in the way of opportunities and of constraints for all prospective land-uses. You then put that to one side.

## Human Needs and Desires

"The greatest possible destruction of the environment, for the greatest possible amount of money?"

Now we have to go back and talk to "Man," as it were. We need to talk to the people, or consumers, of the region who have hired us, and find out their strongest needs and desires, and their most serious problems and concerns. We then return to the description of the region in terms of social phenomena, social processes, and whatever we have in terms of a human ecological model. We wish now to reconstitute this information in terms of unsolved, unfit environments, in terms of the needs and desires on the part of the constituents in the community for better environments, for a better fit between themselves and their environment. I start with the community health index. This allows me to recognize the crises. An area lowest on the community health index allows me to see a community in disintegration. This is an unfit environment, or the people are unable to adapt that environment and/or to adapt themselves.

In the Philadelphia metropolitan region, we have the bottom in a place called South Camden. South Camden is in fact an

absolute behavioral sink. Leadership is absent. Nobody there
wants to be there. Everybody I met there would escape to
some other place if they were able to do so. Horrifying poverty,
human pathology, environmental deprivation, environmental
degradation, environmental and social depravity places Camden
at the very low end of the community health index scale. This
clearly is a problem, both for the people of the region as well as
for the people of this particular community.

We have the fat cats, affluent, comfortable, resolute, dignified,
courageous, whatever you call them at the other end of the community health index scale. These are the people who, according
to the community health index, are inordinately capable of
recognizing and solving problems. They are vigorously healthy
as individuals, as families, and as institutions. Presumably they
constitute a resource to help others to be able to solve the ill fit,
the misfit, the pathology.

We then reconstitute this information of social processes as
problems. We can define problems in terms of unemployment,
or crime, or lice, or crabs, or poor housing, or number of persons
per room, or air pollution, or water pollution. Somebody must
define the problem. The community health index, the index you
derive from vital statistics, allows you not only to define a problem but to locate it spatially and to quantify it. With it, you may
go through the exercise of identifying and locating the problems.
However, the use of an index like "air pollution" is not very accurate. No single factor provides a sufficient method. I find that
this matter of identification of problems can best be done not
only by use of vital statistics–census or environment data–but by
integration through community health indices. Also the employ-

ment of cultural anthropologists to conduct samples and interviews helps. One can do no better than solicit the responses of
the people themselves to their environment. Listen to their own
determination of the degree to which their environments are fit
or unfit for their needs. One identifies structures and elements in
society, and sets up an interview schedule with representatives
of each one of these strata.

The interviews I suggest are oriented toward determination
of the perception of the person questioned to the environment–
both the natural environment and the social environment–and
then the establishment of their response to the environment
as it is presently constituted. Their needs and desires from the
environment need assessment. Once we have this information,
it is possible to formulate plans. Not entirely, but you then have
implications of plans which are revealed by the inadequacies
of the environment and the requirements for change in the
environment, both natural and social, as perceived by the people
who live in this environment, and as reflected in their expression
of needs and desires.

Assessment of need is far from sufficient. One cannot
succeed by simply solving the problems (even if it were possible)
of the present occupants of the region. The future will no doubt
contain many other occupants, about whom we must make
some sort of assumptions, which calls for another group
of advisors. I have depended almost exclusively upon cultural
anthropologists, particularly those concerned with adaptation,
to integrate the information on social phenomena and processes. But the matter of future projection brings in another

group, people who are prepared to make projections on the
housing markets and on transportation; those who foresee
changes in commerce, industry, and so on. To accomplish this,
one has numbers and spatial requirements: there are likely to
be so many more people, who will require so many more
houses; those who have the ability to pay for new houses reside
in such and such a sector. These identify, then, a type of house,
the capability of these people to pay for the land, for the
houses, and to support a density of housing. They identify the
relation of one house to another and to other institutions like
transportation. We begin not only to get dimensions, expressed
as demand for housing, or for recreation, or transportation,
or commerce and industry, but also to get vocational determi-
nants associated with these demands. This information is
assembled, each with its own appropriate hypothesis, into what
we call "growth models."

The assumption is that there will be some aggregate
demand in some intervening time period. "By 1980, the region
under study is likely to have to absorb two million more people,
and these two million more people have the following requirements for housing, industry, commerce, transportation, etc., and
these are the special requirements for each of these demands,"
for example. The two parts—the component of the unsatisfied
needs and desires for the environments and the modifications
required of the existing environment to satisfy the existing
population—are taken, and to this you add the demands of the
future. This permits development of a composite growth model.
It is important to note that each composite growth model is

only as good as the perception of the questionnaire and the interpretation of the social data. We have to be very careful that the problem is not formulated by the planner–which can very easily happen. The formulation of the growth model should derive from a rational interpretation of the statistics, which describe the people and their institutions. It is very important to ensure that the conclusions include the needs and desires of these people. A number of growth models may be made–tens of growth models–because there are going to be different hypotheses about the rate of growth, and the factors that determine not only the rate of growth but also the location of growth may be developed. We then have a number of growth models and hypotheses that are associated with them.

The next problem is one of resource allocation, and the establishment of a value system, both of which are very important. The value system determines the resource allocation. We need to know what resources will be available, and when these resources are in different hands. We need details: which will be disgorged through the federal government, which through the state government, through the private sector, through towns themselves? We must then assess the actual resources that are available. In municipal governments this is seen in the capital budget program. In places where a council of governments exists, we want to see the prospective allocation of resources for the council of governments in the metropolitan region. States make capital budget programs, too. When there is some idea about the kinds of monies that are likely to be disbursed in capital budget programs by various levels of government, I request an idea of the nature of investment by the private sector. This information is generally available from the people who have done the housing market analysis or the transportation market analysis. One must have some quantitative idea of the amounts of resources available.

The most difficult aspect of this exercise is to identify the value system that will pertain. In most cases, the many value systems differ. The value system used by the Bureau of Public Roads is very different from that of the Sierra Club. One can say of the Bureau of Public Roads that they seem to be intent on the greatest possible destruction of the environment, for the greatest possible amount of money, with the least possible amount of social benefit. Presumably, this is quite antithetical to the views of the Sierra Club, which is of course to maintain the maximum amount of wilderness for the maximum gratification of the maximum number of plants and animals.

The solution will vary with respect to the value system, so it is important that the value system is explicit. I would say that one of the most important evolutionary steps in ecological planning is insisting that the value system be explicit. The universal data developed by the natural scientists for the ecological model should be substantial. Every single part of it should be identified by the name of the person who prepared the analysis: "Geology by…, hydrology by…, soils by…, plants by…." All information should be identified, and should be the best available and should be substantial. One should generally be able to get agreement among scientists in that discipline that *this* statement by *that* scientist represents the most current, best statement of the phenomena and processes within the discipline.

The information is explicit, and it is overt. The information in terms of people and places and institutions, the census data, should be as explicit. The interpretation should be explicit. The databank is a constant. We should assume for the purposes of the exercise that it is the latest, best information, and that it is true. The solution to anything, such as the location of a new town, or a sewage treatment plant, or an atomic reactor, or a highway, will vary not as the data varies but only as the value system varies. If the Bureau of Public Roads or the state highway department is required to design a highway between two points, and the citizens form a group concerned with the same highway, the chances are that two quite distinct value systems will arise. Even if we assume that the data that are used to construct the solutions are universally agreed to, given the two value systems, two entirely different solutions will be produced. It is important to realize what the value system is that generates the solution.

The ecological planning report must state that the plan is for an investment by a unit, for example a unit of government or of the private sector. All such units have value systems, which need to be explicit. It may be important, for example, to have open space above all other things, or to have pure air above all other things; alternatively, it may be important to have high employment levels above all other things. Of course, each one of these values will affect other values. The man who says "I insist on full employment" is in effect saying he will let the environment degrade. He is prepared to accept a degeneration of the environment because he insists that full employment is more important than conservation. One can develop an established, explicit value statement in which it says, for example, that this institution with this particular value system is prepared to make this amount of investment for this particular end. Then you make a resource allocation, a process which again is particularly suited for the computer. It is a beautiful thing for the computer to do; it can do it very cleverly and very fast. You simply identify all of the factors of the environment that the consumer requires, his capability for realizing his goals—in terms of the amount of money he can pay for land or investment in land for development—and you then ask the computer to find that place which meets all of the requirements of that consumer, and to allocate that resource for the future. The growth model is like a bank, where you have all of this money, and all of the consumers and their ability to be able to achieve their objective of finding the most fit environment. You simply allocate consumers to available resources as a result of when you lay them in, development after development in small time increments. You show alternative forms of urban or metropolitan or regional growth as the result of months of investment over periods of time in response to specific consumers with specific needs and desires from the environment, with a specific value system. In the end, you show the alternative forms of growth, alternative fashions of development, you display them to the consumer, because the consumer must choose. The consumer may be a regional government or a city government. It may be a private landowner who is prepared to make a new town. He is interested then in alternative patterns and he must finally express his preference.

In the good and proper world, all of this, which of course does not now exist, and probably never will, should be commonplace. We now have the technology, and presumably we now have the intelligence, so that every single part of the United States, at every single scale, very well could be subject to an ecological inventory.

We might use our satellite capability, our capability to put remote sensors in high-altitude aircraft, use high-level aerial photography, and supplement remote observation with ground-truth. We might be explicit about our degrees of approximation, of accuracy, of discrimination of the continent—every natural region within the continent to yield an entire ecological inventory. There is no reason why these data should not be digitized. The information, in many cases, can be digitized from the source, from the satellite right into the computer, and stored. In my good and proper world, all of these data would be available to anybody in public libraries. If I wish, I should be able to go to the computer terminal at the public library and ask it to display for me, in coordinates which I enumerate, the bedrock geology, surficial geology, physiography, hydrology, soils, plants, and animals. Moreover, I would want to have these data interpreted for my particular uses, i.e. depth to bedrock, seasonal high water table—I don't want to have a wet basement. I would assess the availability of enough water, for example, to have a single-family house with its own well on the property. I would like to identify the rocks in terms of their compressive strength for foundations–particularly for the architects. I would like to have all these data interpreted. I would like to have them displayed, and also to get hard copy. Why can't I put a quarter in the machine and walk away with not only the television monitor display of the data I want, but also hard copy that I can take home and ponder? Moreover, I would like to have in this public library, as in all public libraries in my utopian circumstance, the possibility of having convergence programs available–computer programs of the sort that my students and I use, where one simply asks for any region under study, to find the convergence of all the factors that I identify as most propitious for any need. That is, I would like to say, "I want to find a location for a second home. I want it to be not more than one hour distance from Philadelphia, on land that costs not more than $5,000 an acre, on which I can have an on-site septic tank and an on-site well. I want it to be a mixed mesophytic forest in which I can expect to see deer and the red hawk, and I would like to be nearest to the flyway." I would like to be able to identify all factors that represent some sort of a utopia for me, and ask a convergence program to show me where these places are. There is no reason why we should not take these steps. The accumulation of all of this information and the analysis using convergence programs requires no higher intelligence; if it did, I would not be able to describe it!

All I describe here really is only the aggregation and the interpretation of, in many cases, available published data. The data are integrated and made available through digitizing and computer display techniques. In my good and proper world we would be able to do something more. We would be able to analyze other projects which were made either in the public or private domains. Let us consider the Bureau of Public Roads again; say that the state highway department has proposed a highway. It would be very nice to ask to have displayed the geology, geomorphology, hydrology, plants, animals, and so forth on that alignment. With the information in front of us, we might then be able to ask what are the implications, what is the environmental impact of a highway as proposed upon that place. Not only the natural environment, but the social environment needs concern us too. It would also be very nice to say, "I would like to change the value system. I would like to see a solution which is responsive to my value system." Let us say that my value system dictates that the most important consideration for the highway is recognition of community integrity in this region. People live in definable areas–they believe themselves to live in a definable area, they converge on institutions–and if the highway goes right through the middle of their space, it will in fact disrupt their community integrity. My value system would say, "First of all, the highway must recognize and respect the community integrity. My value system insists on the amenity of the area, its quiet, dignity, etc." I would enumerate my social value system and say, "All right now, find a solution which is responsive to my social value system." Such information from data sets should be available to everybody. If such a system were in place, planning would become an overt, explicit, replicable process. It could become a public process, in which anybody would be able under these circumstances to examine any proposal in the public domain, or even in the private domain. We must be able to examine the data being used to find the solutions, the weighting of the factors which have been used in finding the solution, and therefore the value system which has been used. With this information, we will be able to offer alternative solutions based upon alternative value systems. Of course, the final resolution of land use lies at the polls, where different people with different values have the opportunity of voting for solutions responsive to different values. In democracy, presumably, the largest number of votes wins, and that is the solution reflecting the value system of the majority.

## Ecological Planning in the Future
"We should have some sort of resolution to complete the American Revolution"

Such planning is actually possible. Of course, it is not being done now. In fact, nowhere do I know that all of the elements in this ecological planning process I have described have been employed. I myself have employed, either in teaching or in prac-tice, every single step, but in no place that I am aware have all of the elements been used in a single planning process. Yet no new intelligence is required. People exist who know how to do every single part. There is not any reason why all of this should not be, in fact, the prevailing planning process. Within the context of a legislative process it can be realized. Most private planning done by consultants like me operates on the basis of consent. A client, whoever it is, employs a planner. The planner has to be most responsive to his client and the ability of his community to realize the plan. The plan itself has no power at all. This is a very salutary thing. All becomes very different when one talks with the community, which has, after all, through the Ninth and Fourteenth Amendments to the U.S. Constitution, the moral responsibility of looking after the welfare of its citizens. The community has the power of law to exercise police power to ensure the health and welfare of citizens. I would think that as a result of the Environmental Protection Act and the Environmental Protection Agency, there is now a great possibility on the part of planners, both in the public and in the private domain, to organize human and ecological planning in such a way that it is oriented to regulation. That is, as one goes through the exercise of ground and surface water, it should be possible to write regulations to insist upon performance standards for development to ensure the perpetuation of the social values represented in the quality and quantity and the spatial distribution of water.

It should be possible to identify certain areas where there are hazards to life and health, for example from volcanism, earthquakes, seismic activity, avalanches, hurricanes, mudslides, or flooding. There are floods now, and obviously many people will drown in these floods, because every American believes he has an inalienable right to build in the floodplain and to be drowned. I believe that this should be seen as a special kind of madness that falls within the police power of government.

People really should be prohibited from drowning. It is a public embarrassment to have to haul these people off, when they survive, to the high schools, and feed them, declare a national emergency, and then help them clear the mud out of the basement. Clearly, where hazards for life and health exist, regulation that restricts land use in areas that are unsuitable for human occupancy or habitation is appropriate. I believe it will become increasingly important that all planning of the sort we describe should be oriented toward the capability of the use of government to enforce plans by identification of phenomena and processes where there are hazards to life and health. Where land use is likely to lead to a loss of a unique or scarce or irreplaceable resource, where it is likely there will be a loss of a high social value, the government should be used to enforce appropriate plans. All of the data which I am talking about in the ecological planning process can be reconstituted within each category and oriented toward the formulation of ecological ordinances or ecological regulations. Whether written at the federal, state, county, or the municipal level, it would seem to me that the people themselves can utilize their political powers to write regulations to prohibit "development" in those areas where there is a hazard to life and health, or where there is a likelihood of the loss of irreplaceable, scarce, unique, or valuable resources.

I emphasize here the regulatory side, but I want to complement these comments with the positive or affirmative side. Employment of intrinsic suitabilities and their reconstitution into zoning maps should identify areas that are unsuitable for certain land uses for explicit reasons. Performance standards could be established. In an aquifer recharge area, for example, the appropriate rule might state that a builder may do anything he likes, just so long as he does not diminish the amount of recharge, and does not cause a deterioration in the quality of the water which is being recharged. This then is an example of a performance specification. If somebody plans to build a regional shopping center in this area, and requires ten acres of asphalt, the local permit granters do not say he cannot do it. Rather, they simply say that if he does continue, he must collect all the surface water, which will run off the parking area; he must treat that surface water, such that it attains an acceptable level of water quality; and then he must build an injection well to restore the water to the aquifer. If the regional shopping center can afford the investment, then it may build on the aquifer recharge area. If it cannot, an alternative must be sought, somewhere not in an aquifer recharge area.

Restrictive regulatory devices can be used, but I think the affirmative ones are as important. To be able to grow a community we must have a planning process that documents that particular areas are, by definition, extremely fit for particular land uses. If the community seeks areas that should be developed with low-density residential housing with on-site septic tanks and wells, these areas are suitable. For intermediate density housing, with public sewers and water, these other areas are extremely propitious. Regional shopping centers are best put here, industries of different types there, and recreational uses by type here.

This affirmative form should become a zoning map. Zoning is a political decision by which segregation is enforced, and damn dullness ensues. We create the dullest possible residential environment through the present political instrument of zoning. I think if we were to seriously embrace the intrinsic suitability model, the outcome would be different. Instead of single uses, we would develop multiple, compatible, coexisting land-uses. We would not have segregation; instead we would have fitness.

I am absolutely obsessed by this method. It astonishes me that I can actually survive and receive money for provision of services for a planning method so fundamentally simple. I really operate here at the level of the last, best, nineteenth-century natural science. Nothing of the sort of planning I envision and promote requires any fancy late-twentieth-century science. Yet my methods are not widely used. They are considered to be on a threshold, an incredible novelty. But my ideas are theoretically supportable. If Darwin is right and the surviving organism is fit for the environment, and Henderson is right that the environment does in fact offer every possible opportunity for every prospective consumer, then the business of the accomplishment of fitness requires the organism not only to find the most fit environment and adapt that environment and itself, but also to do so dynamically and continuously. The environment changes as a result of the fitting, and a continuous necessity to find the best environment is created. To adapt that environment and to adapt oneself is an incessant imperative. I believe these ideas can be institutionalized into the planning process. I think such a planning process oriented toward "adaptive fitness" necessarily would have the components I have described. It seems to me a marvelously open method, but every single part of it can be improved. The natural science can be improved, the data can be improved, the understanding of process can be improved, the models can be improved, the interactions between the models can be improved. Every single part of every aspect of the planning process I describe can be improved. There is a fantastic amount of utility and value in existing knowledge, integrated and actually utilized in the performance of this ecological planning.

I have a little dream—I have a lot of fantasies. My best fantasy is that we decide here and now that we have to have some sort of resolution about the face of America, certainly for 1976. In the Bicentennial, we should have some sort of resolution to complete the American Revolution. We know it is the most successful social revolution—in fact, probably the only successful social revolution that has occurred. Without doubt, the physical adaptation that has been accomplished by this American experiment is its worst indictment. That is the part that requires the greatest remedy. The remedy is simple. Why don't we simply implement an ecological inventory of the whole continent? Why don't we have a sample survey of the whole population, heavily weighted toward youth? Why don't we find out from them their needs and desires, both in the physical environment and in the social environment? Why don't we then make alternative future models of the face of America, showing the pattern and distribution of urbanization, reflecting all of the variability of environments and the variability of choices? Then, simply make the resolution of this a matter for the 1976 bicentennial year, so that, at the conclusion of this birthday, we have some idea what the face of the land of the free and the home of the brave should look like at some future time. The Revolution then will be rather more complete than it is now. I think this change in the face of America will involve ecological planning of the sort I have described, and I certainly commend it to your attention.

Sketch of McHarg by an anonymous artist.

# Conversation

Ian L. McHarg

"We have to be very careful that the problem is not
formulated by the planner."

**You mentioned Lawrence Henderson. Might you tell us more about his work?**

Lawrence J. Henderson was a great man. He was unappreciated at Harvard. He never advanced further than Associate Professor of Biology. He wrote a memorable book, called the *Fitness of the Environment*.[1] I think he was a great man, certainly comparable to Darwin. He must be considered complementary to Darwin. Darwin simply claimed that the surviving organism is fit for the environment, but he said nothing about the environment's fitness for the organism. Henderson said the evolving environment was adapted by life to make the environment more fit for life. The reciprocity in this matter of the fitness of the environment for life, he said, is at least as important a consideration as the fitness of the organism to the environment. I apologize for paraphrasing Henderson. I recommend you read George Wald as the greatest exponent of Henderson. Wald wrote a beautiful introduction to the recent edition of *The Fitness of the Environment*.[2] Nevertheless, I think I can justify paraphrasing him.

Henderson said the actual current environment consists of the fittest possible abode for life–every form of life that has, does, or will exist. He elaborated on this by identifying the characteristics of the abundance of oxygen, hydrogen, carbon–to which George Wald added nitrogen. Henderson then examined the characteristics of water, specific heat, buoyancy of ice, water's properties as a solvent, carbonic acid, the oceans, and the atmosphere. He concluded, based on their abundance and their characteristics, that this planet is indeed the fittest possible abode for life. There is a certain amount of circularity in his argument, obviously, but he sees reciprocity between life and its environment. Of all possible conditions of gases and matter, those present in oxygen, carbon, nitrogen, hydrogen, water, and so on, do offer an extraordinarily favorable environment for life. This environment has been substantially modified by life.

He goes on to say that the atmosphere was made by life; it is in fact the product of the exhalations of the entire metabolism of all life over all time, which has given us the present atmosphere. According to Henderson, in these homeostatic, thermostatic responses in temperature and other factors, the atmosphere exhibits the attributes of an organism. Moreover, the same is true of the oceans, with respect to their temperature, alkalinity and acidity, and the balance of carbon dioxide. The ocean, too, exhibits the self-regulatory characteristics of an organism. Henderson was reaffirming the fitness of the environment for life. It is remarkable that this book was written in 1911. It is a pre-atomic book, yet Wald claims it is still one of the most important books.

### What is the relationship between thermodynamic and artistic creativity?

I certainly am no authority on this subject, but I do have some ideas. My sense is that creativity in any process, certainly in any biological process, involves three interdependent points. Obviously something in the system must be capable of entrapping energy and/or matter temporarily on its path toward entropy. The chloroplast traps light to an astonishing degree. The chloroplast simply is a device by which the plant can capture solar energy into its being, and transmute it into that essential proper self, at least temporarily. This period of arrestment of the energy from origin to entropy is that period in which the ordering occurs that permits all life to thrive or persist.

The next point that would seem to be coequally important to this fundamental creativity is apperception: the ability of any system—social, natural, physical, biological—to be able to perceive energy not only as energy but as information, and to transmute that information into meaning. Indeed, creative photosynthesis requires it. A plant must be heliotropic—that is, it must seek sunlight—and must be able to perceive the visible range of sunlight that it needs. The plant must be able to use sunlight in photosynthesis.

That same ability will hold true for me. I must be able to perceive sunlight as sunlight, to perceive that sunlight warms me, and to transmute this sun energy into information. I am warmed and interpret the meaning, which causes me to act: to either have a beer or a swim, or to take off my jacket and open my collar. This ability of apperception seems to me the realm in which humans have the greatest potential for creativity. We are uniquely able to perceive the environment as energy, as information, and to transmute this into meaning.

If this is the unique creative ability of Man, then perhaps one should see the artist, the painter, and the sculptor in these terms. One might ask the artist about his ability to see the environment as energy, capable of transmuting information and meaning. I would ask a painter first of all, "What are you saying?" He may say it representatively or abstractly. I am not interested in how he says it, but I am interested in what he says. I am very interested in the adaptive value of what he says. If the Renaissance constitutes a great efflorescence of art, but the understanding of the environment and the suggestions of how to relate to the environment are erroneous, as was true of Renaissance art, the art may be great in terms of representation and in terms of evocation, but in terms of adaptive value, it is a calamity.

The Renaissance view of Man and Nature in my own view was calamitous. Its insistence that Nature must be subordinate to Man accounts for all of the impoverishment, which exists in the Mediterranean world now and will persist for some time. If the artist is able to perceive meaning in the environment which has adaptive value, and can convey this meaning to people who are then responsive to this understanding, the artist is in fact thermodynamically creative.[3]

**If social evolution is a process of creative fitting, how do you account for social pathology?**

Of course, there is an enormous amount of pathology, such as slums. My answer would have to be that these are all evidence of some misfit. Something in the system, whether at the level of cell, tissue, organ, organism, or ecosystem, or whether as an individual, family, or institution, is misfit.

The simplest misfit to examine would be physiological assaults that exceed the capacity for recovery of the system. Many abound; we live, after all, in an environment of poisons: lead, hydrocarbon, noise, female hormones in steak, and nutritional additives. Some are clearly very serious physiological stresses. One may recover from these insults, or escape from them. In other cases it is quite impossible. A steady diet with intolerable levels of lead is a serious physiological burden for many. They are unable to escape from these stressful environments.

This is just as true of psychological stresses. All of the experiments on animal behavior, for example with rats, show that pathology is associated with rank. The dominant animal has virtually no disease whatsoever. The immediate subordinate animals, comparable to vice presidents in human society, are rotten with heart disease and kidney disease. Immediately below that are animals that have even higher dimensions of stress pathology; they move from physical pathology to social pathology. Finally, at the bottom, are the catatonic ones.[4]

In the absence of the ability to escape competition, there seems to be some correlation between rank order and physical, psychological, and social disease. In human society, often there are opportunities for people to escape. The face-to-face encounters between the president and the vice president may be terribly stressful for the vice president. Yet the encounter between the vice president and his laundryman or his servant or his wife or his sons may be able to overcome the stress engendered by his subordinate position. Nonetheless, many people in society are so low and have so little means of escape that they are subjected to an astonishing amount of stress pathology.

Of course, the same is true in the social realm. There are environments where it is impossible to find employment, never mind a responsible role. I think it is essential to happiness and creativity to enjoy some social significance in one's own eyes,

and in the eyes of one's associates, to be able to have the dignity
I see as a precondition of health.

I suppose my answer is that evidence of a misfit is wherever
you find some physical, social, or mental pathology. The misfit
may be the presence of stress, but it also has to be associated with
the inability of the system under discussion to accomplish remedy.

One of the more remarkable things I saw in my life's experience was to see prisoners of war liberated. All of these were
subjected to the same indignity of the spirit. All suffered humili-
ating conditions and had enormous difficulty in keeping clean
and warm. Malnutrition was rampant. Yet coming out of these
camps were people whose dignity was absolutely and totally
unassailed. Some came out clean and totally unscathed, while
others emerged craven. I would dearly love to know, what are
the preconditions for making a child into a man or a woman
who has this inviolable dignity? What is it that gives some sense
of what it is that allows them to seek problems and solve them?

## How do you keep maps current?

It is extremely difficult to ensure that maps are current. One
goes through an enormously laborious exercise identifying all
of the attributes of the region, phenomena and process. Many
of these are dynamic and subject to change. If it is possible to
transfer the information from map information to digitized information, which has the form of storage in tape or punch cards,
then currency is no longer a problem. As changes occur, one
takes out the appropriate cards, and enters the changes. One of
the limitations of this is that the printout one gets from a com-

puter that uses only typewriter keys is despicable looking. When
you think about the beauty, elegance, and legibility of the map
that one ingests into the computer, when you see the printout,
it is a matter of some despair. Nonetheless, although it is not
attractive, the information is all there. It is possible by using a
computer, a digital scanner, and a printout, to be able to keep
this ecological and land-use information current.

Land-use really is, of course, dynamic. Look at land-use
maps historically, and you will see that areas that were intensively urbanized are no longer urbanized. A map of New Jersey
in the early and mid-1800s shows very intense and uniform
urbanization all over southern New Jersey. There is virtually
none any more. An enormous area of farmland in New England,
which was intensively cultivated, now reveals itself only in stone
walls and woodlands. I would say there is probably more land
going out of agriculture into forestry simply by old-field succession than there is going out of agriculture and into urbanization.
There are abandoned quarries, docks, and industrial buildings.
Much land lies in dereliction, some of it then becomes vacant.
Some of it is re-urbanized, and some eventually reverts to
open space. I do not have the data, although Jean Gottman in
his book *Megalopolis* has some quite remarkable figures on the
reversions of urban land.[5]

What do you think of the effects of human overpopulation
on the environment?
Overpopulation is a situation where there simply are too many
people, but population numbers are inevitably related to many

things. Barry Commoner wrote a beautiful book on this subject.[6] At one point, he compared the clothing that his parents wore with that which he wore. He remarked that his father was well dressed and tended to wear linen or wool shirts, and leather shoes. His mother tended to wear silk, cotton, and linen. On examination, he found that he wore clothes mostly of synthetic fibers. He did not infer that he was any better dressed than his mother or father, but there was a profound difference. To grow flax to produce linen is not stressful for the environment. Sheep produce wool, and they are marginally stressful on the environment—they can be managed not to be excessively stressful on the environment. Silkworms are certainly stressful to mulberry trees, but not necessarily to their whole environment. His parents dressed very well indeed, without putting extraordinary stress on the environment.

However, Commoner and people like him are dressed now essentially in synthetic fibers, which are stressful to the environment in ways that are multiples of silkworms, flax, cotton, and wool. Processes to produce synthetics require enormous quantities of energy in order to fuel them. They produce products that are not any better than the preceding ones. The effluents they produce are non-biodegradable. They are inordinately stressful to the environment.

If only we operated the other way around: instead of the thought that commodities represent well-being, we decided that well-being was an objective. We might ask what the pre-conditions for well-being are. If one of the preconditions were to minimize the stress on both the natural environment and on the human environment, I believe we could aspire to a higher and more real quality of life. Perhaps the world could even support higher population numbers. We certainly could improve the quality of life with present numbers.

The essential thing is that services are not stressful to the environment. The provision of compassion, intelligence, education, medical services, justice, or even an attractive working and living environment need not be stressful. Of course, there are limits to numbers, but we should be concerned with the well-being of those numbers now. How can we manage our affairs to effect the least stress on the environment? How can we change our concept of well-being from a measurement based on commodity flow to one based on the quality of life? Might we not emphasize services which are ennobling of both the provider of services and the recipient? Such revised behaviors certainly should allow us more tolerance in dealing with present societies. Even larger numbers of people in the future might be supported.

You say that the final resolution lies at the polls. Do you really have faith in politics to help us?

The vote always depends on who is voting, which depends on the constituency. The votes should arbitrate any decision. Perhaps we might start at the top and work down. If there were custodians for the world atmosphere, stratosphere, the Van Allen Belt, for the oceans, for the major denizens that transgress natural boundaries, it would be very nice. We have, of course, no such custodians.

If there were an international legal force that protected all of our Van Allen Belt, our stratosphere and atmosphere, our ocean and its major life forms, then we might invoke some national responsibility for the denizens and the people within national boundaries. Some sort of Bill of Rights for nature would be appropriate. A lawyer in Islip, New York, Victor J. has claimed that implicit in the Ninth and Fourteenth Amendments to the Constitution is a statement that guarantees the right to the quality of the environment. If it is not now explicit, perhaps it should be made explicit, that Americans should have an inalienable right to pure air and clean water, and that defenses against assaults on the environment are crucial. These aggressions are just as lethal as attacks by knife and gun and fist.

This would then bring us down to lower regions. States should also have the power to interpret with finer discrimination some bill of rights for the environment at their level. I suggest operations at the level of single towns. Townships should be able to write their own ecological ordinances to regulate the deployment of their resources; on the assumption that the town itself constitutes a social value system of the town. We cannot really pose the problem, as the activities of the town of course influence the environment of the town, which will have some influence on the state.

I suppose I have no final solution to this. It must depend upon the vote. The problem of resolution is not whether or not one wishes to depend on the vote to make the data and the value system explicit, but how to define the constituency. Who really should be involved in the decision?

I insist, however, that the basis for making decisions about the environment be overt and explicit. The method to come to solutions should be replicable, and the sleight-of-hand, fiction, inaccurate information, gossip, and political chicanery that constitutes the basis for most decisions should decidedly be replaced by a public, open, logical, flexible, and explicit planning process.

Notes

1  Lawrence J. Henderson, *The Fitness of the Environment* (Boston: Beacon
   Press, 1958; republished New York: Peter Smith Publishing, 1987). McHarg's
   recognition of the validity of Henderson's conclusions here independent
   of their similarity to I. V. Vernadsky's (1863–1945) ideas (*The Biosphere,*
   New York: Springer-Verlag, 1998) and to the Gaia hypothesis (J. E.
   Lovelock, *Ages of Gaia,* New York: Norton, 1988) is truly remarkable.
2  Wald was a Harvard professor of biology from 1948–77. His introduction to
   *The Fitness of the Environment* appears in the 1958 Beacon Press edition.
3  See film with Ian McHarg, *Multiply and Subdue the Earth,* a PBS broadcast
   on January 1969 illustrates McHarg's most important ideas.
4  McHarg adds before this last comment, "They tend to be marginally
   homosexual. Further down the social hierarchy we get fully homosexual
   rats." He is probably referring to the general adaptive syndrome first
   noted by Hans Seyle in his seminal 1936 article in the journal *Nature.*
   The American Psychiatric Association has not considered homosexuality
   pathological among humans since 1973, when it was removed from the
   second edition of the Diagnostic and Statistical Manual of Mental
   Disorders. McHarg may have been influenced by a 1972 research study by
   Ingebog Ward, showing that pre-natal stress led to homosexual behavior
   among the male offspring of the stressed rats. While his mention of
   homosexuality as social pathology may be obsolete, McHarg's suggestion
   that stress leads to social pathology is still valid. Seyle and others
   since have shown that stress in dense populations of rats leads to social
   pathologies such as infanticide, cannibalism, and aggression, even if
   food is plentiful.
5  Jean Gottman, *Megalopolis* (Baltimore: Johns Hopkins University Press,
   1990).
6  McHarg probably refers here to Barry Commoner, *The Closing Circle*
   (New York: Random House, 1971).

# POND WATER

Ian L. McHarg, c. 1980, unpublished

To test

a new microscope

a drop of pond water,

A teeming world,

creatures shooting across the slide,

some passing through others.

A rotifer with a propellor

in the middle of its head,

metasynchronized cilia.

Improbable,

as are they all

living out lives

lasting minutes

Are we so different?

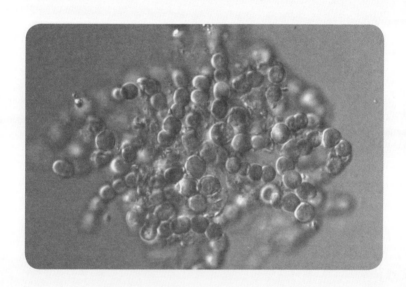

*Nostoc gunnera,* a cyanobacterium, is the ancestor to the algal
chloroplast and is capable of the formation of food from light and
air. Cyanobacteria photosynthesize, produce nitrogen compounds and
help make soil for the rest of the biosphere. This *Nostoc* filament taken
from the glands of the flowering plant *Gunnera manicata* ("poor man's
umbrella") was photographed by Rita Kolchinslei Berson.

# "The algae will laugh."

McHarg and the Second Law of Thermodynamics
Dorion Sagan

I always try to write on the principle of the iceberg. There is
seven-eighths of it underwater for every part that shows.
–Ernest Hemingway

If you write a sentence and you don't like it, but that's what you
wanted to say, you say it again in another way. Once you start
doing it and you find how difficult it is, you get interested. You
have it, then you lose it again, and then you get it again. You
have to change to stay the same.
–William De Kooning

When I was a college student, ideological identification was a sort of political
shorthand, showing you were committed–even if it was to the anarchist non-
cause of nihilism! In this environment, I had two stock answers. One was that
I was a "Gnostic" (linguistically, at least, the opposite of an agnostic, "one who
knows"). The second was that I was a "geographical determinist." Although
delivered tongue-in-cheek at the time, I see now that both are largely true.
And both deal with energy, that changeable currency (stored also in atoms,
as World War II graphically demonstrated) studied by thermodynamics and
highlighted in McHarg's theory of creativity.

Although McHarg disparages as "calamitous" the legacy of the Renaissance–presumably because it raised humanity, mentally but not physically out
of the landscape–he is himself a sort of Renaissance Man. Better yet, a Universal Man. He freely admits his ignorance, so he cunningly assembles a variety of
scientists, each of whom specializes in a different aspect of landscape analysis,
in order to create artistically a representation of the human living situation

as completely as possible. McHarg wants us to view deeply into space and time, the context of our potential dwelling, in order to optimize our chances of bringing it into accord with the Earth that has sustained our ancestors and, we hope, will sustain our descendants. It is from this holism, I believe, that his interest in energy derives.

The first law of thermodynamics tells us energy never disappears, and the second tells us energy inevitably falls from a usable to a non-usable state. Energy as emanation from the sun cycles through all ecosystems, empowering the organization we see in self-maintaining, growing, and reproducing life, including civilization. But energy is a double-edged sword. Exuberance is beauty, yes, and the palace of solar excess leads to our earthly activity, pleasures, and wisdom. Yet the solar excess must be channeled carefully and spent wisely, or it will burn a hole in our collective pocket, the pocket of humanity, which, McHarg claims, is "the most endangered species." We are endangered precisely because of our excess, our wealth, our rapid spread over the last million years from a few hairy woodland hunters to more than six billion modern humans with cell phones. "Power," Nietzsche quipped, "makes [us] stupid": like a wonderful neighborhood restaurant that becomes a lousy fast-food chain, tool-using humanity has spread to the ends of the Earth without proper regard for the underlying landscape by which we are, in the final analysis, geographically determined. McHarg, advocating for example that developers collect and treat surface water displaced by asphalt if they are going to build a shopping center, tries to redress this over-expenditure. Looking to nature and common sense, McHarg presents us with a less stupid path.

As an artistically inclined writer at work for the last eight years on a book on the thermodynamics of natural flow systems, I wake up when McHarg defines creativity as "the employment of energy and matter to raise matter and energy to higher levels of order." What is striking about his definition is that it shows creativity to be more than human. The fact is that beautiful, complex structures—structures that perfectly marry form to function, and forms that moreover can be and have been mistaken to be the result of conscious artifice or design—occur naturally outside the realm of both life and art. (Scientists should know better than to make this mistake!) What the beautiful nonliving structure-building processes—for they, like we living beings, are really more process than thing—have in common is that all occur in areas of energy flow. Energy flow, in turn, predictably occurs where there are gradients. A gradient is a natural difference of physical quantity; for example, a measurable difference across a distance in pressure or temperature. As nature abhors a vacuum, so too does it, in the phrase of Montana ecologist Dr. Eric D. Schneider, abhor a gradient.[1] Indeed, nature's abhorrence of a gradient over ecological scales is another, broader statement of the second law of thermodynamics. Nature abhors a gradient: this means that, when and where possible, particulate matter in the area of a gradient will come together, sometimes in quite fascinatingly complex formations, to reduce ambient gradients. Examples of such natural creativity include spinning hurricanes and tornadoes, which reduce an atmospheric pressure gradient; psychedelic Belousov-Zhabotinskii reactions, which spin out French curves and change colors as they reduce a chemical gradient; and hexagons that form when silicone and sperm whale oil are heated, called Bénard cells, which reduce a temperature gradient.

Thermodynamically, we humans, and all life forms, are a similar sort of system. The vast majority of our proto-living ancestors likely reproduced with a distinct lack of high fidelity. But they were nonetheless selves, selfish in the way that "Whirlpool," a giant eddy downstream of Niagara Falls that is so continuous it has been baptized with a name, is selfish. The alert reader will be reminded that hurricanes are also, and for the same reason, given a name: they have, however fleeting, a recognizable identity. Likewise, proto-life likely

consisted of transparent cell-like bags of chemicals becoming temporarily
more complex as they reduced ambient gradients. The bags were amphiphi-
lic, made of molecules that kept oily, colloidal substances in and water out.
The need for naturally occurring complex systems to be near gradients is
one reason that some scientists believe early life arose in the proximity of gas
vents in the crust of early Earth. Such areas, similar to geysers and extreme
environments today, where the ancient bacteria known as archae (or archae-
bacteria) dwell in sulfide hot springs, are sites of the temperature and chemical gradients that are used to "fund" complexity.

One thus must agree with McHarg's intuition that creativity "always
shows the tendency to move from a greater to a lesser randomness, from simplicity to complexity, from uniformity to diversity, from instability toward
dynamic equilibrium, from a low to a high number of species, from a low to a
higher number of symbioses," and that "creativity is not [just] some attribute
of painters and sculptors."[2] Indeed, creativity appears spontaneously in
regions of thermodynamic flow. Life is distinct from hurricanes, twister tornadoes, and chemical clocks because it has happened upon a means of maintain-
ing itself as a stable mode of gradient degradation. This mode—we call it
reproduction—connects what Charles Darwin's grandfather, Erasmus, called
the "organum," the parent form, to its offshoots. The more things change,
as De Kooning suggests above, the more they stay the same. Underneath this
cliché is an artistic and scientific insight—the production, via processes of gra-
dient-reduction, of stable, creative, and entirely natural thermodynamic iden-
tities. The butterfly dies, but before it does so it lays eggs that become the cat-
erpillar larvae and pupae and—surprise—it then metamorphoses to the winged
form. The life cycle is just that—a cycle, one intimately connected to
a very specific environment laced with gradients that the butterfly uses but
doesn't use up.

We *Homo sapiens* too are thermodynamic systems that need to use our environment wisely, which, for us, means not to use it up. McHarg is the understated master at moving this agenda out from beneath its cloud of worrisome longing into the clear light of rational understanding. C. P. Snow famously said that not to understand the second law of thermodynamics is equivalent to not having read Shakespeare.[3] But he was wrong: it is worse. If we fail to read Shakespeare we are individually threatened with relative ignorance, while if we do not understand the ways of energy we collectively are threatened with extinction. Freud, another one who thought much on energy, in his study on wit remarks that the reason we laugh at slapstick or animals is because we perceive as ridiculous the difference between the energy expended and that necessary to do the job: the energetic animal jumps around too much and is thus as laughable as the person who thinks too little.[4] But the animal of human society—a monster out of control who is yet nothing else than us—as a connected open thermodynamic system—is rapaciously biting the global environment that feeds it. "The algae will laugh. 'Next time no brains,' they will say, and evolution will proceed into some lovely new expression."[5] Let us hope for our own sakes that McHarg here is right when he says modestly that he is just a "simple minded" landscape architect—and not instead giving us a futuristic flash, one final example of the elegance of his Scottish intuition.

Notes

1   Eric D. Schneider and Dorion Sagan, *Into the Cool: Energy Flow, Thermodynamics and Life* (Chicago: University of Chicago Press, 2005).

2   Ian McHarg, "The Theory of Creative Fitting," in this volume, 21.

3   Snow, C. P., *The Two Cultures and a Second Look* (Cambridge, UK: Cambridge University Press, 1969).

4   Freud, Sigmund, *The Joke and Its Relation to the Unconscious* (New York: Penguin, 2003).

5   Ian McHarg, "The Theory of Creative Fitting," this volume, 21.

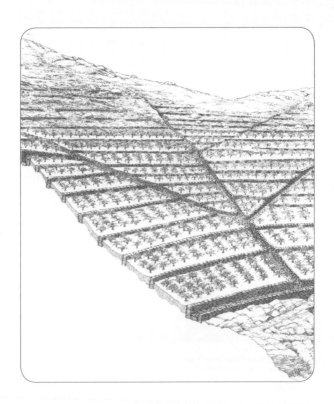

Agricultural terraces; an Earth scene modified by men.

# "We ask them to group together all these independent spectral views of the universe into one whole system."

Biosphera, Global Knowledge for Community Design
Ramon Folch

What does the work of Ian McHarg and his admonition to "design with nature" mean? What is nature? Like all obvious concepts, it defies simple definition. Nothing is more difficult to define than the obvious. Self-evident referents become premises for everything else; rather than define them, they simply must be assumed. Just because Nature, Life, Death, Organism, and the like seem obvious does not mean they are not complex. The concept "nature" is certainly a complex idea. Everything around us is "natural" because all things are material. Cities, for example, are "natural artifacts" of the human species. If cities were not to be recognized as natural, than neither would birds' nests, ant farms, termite mounds, beaver dams, or even spider webs. And if all is natural, then everything is part of nature. And if all is nature, nature is all and therefore cannot even be defined.

What McHarg opposed in his dictum to design with nature was the pretentious "design against nature." Misconceptions have prevailed since the Renaissance: the tendency to consider culture to be outside nature, and natural phenomena to be lower than culture. This we consider erroneous. Culture is an intellectual construction based on nature. In the same way, architecture begins with nature. We humans always build in nature and alongside of something. Our constructions are membranes that, like all interfaces, modulate gradients of energy and matter.

To build is to construct boundaries, barriers, interfaces, and permeable membranes that preserve ecophysiological differences. Differences in temperature, light, quantity of water vapor, sound, and other measurable properties of an environment are maintained by our constructs. Boundaries, membranes, walls, fences, and other physical limits may also protect privacy. This might be considered a form of coexistence differential, a permeable border that maintains separation between different egos. Viewed this way, architecture becomes a subspecialty of biology, just as medicine is of zoology. Recognition of architecture and medicine as subfields shows us the particular extremes that display the anthropocentric vision of the world. Both deal with energy flow and irreducibly concrete material transformation and reveal, above all, the biased manner in which we live in and describe nature.

Surrounded by the limiting but permeable border is the modified environment, and beyond the membrane is the environment per se. Which of these, the interior or the exterior, is really most affected by the architectural act? Both equally, it seems; and both deserve, we believe, similar attention. The paradox, nevertheless, is that architecture often creates internal environments that are in serious conflict with their greater surroundings. Architecture is then to a large extent a self-contradictory set of actions, particularly when it ventures explicitly into the greater environment beyond the building and into the landscape. Landscape architecture, and even more environmental protection and natural resource management reverse the membrane because they attempt to organize the "out-of-doors." In reality they blur the interface because they dilute the membrane. They restore the environment to its original status, which seems very good to me. Landscape architecture then constructs not "alongside of" but "in the heart of," alongside of spaces in which gradients cease to be conflicts.

To construct "in the heart of" we must "be inside." In this manner, we transform the constructed membrane from an abrupt limit to a benign boundary. Even more, we pacify the inside by the cessation of hostilities with the outside. In this way, the inside-outside differences are no longer the steep gradients that generate conflicts, the "reductive misfit revealed in pathology," as McHarg calls it. Gentler gradients can be maintained in the absence of hostility. If we interpret McHarg he might agree with us that architecture would always be of the landscape, and the local landscape would always be represented in the interior environment. We arrive in this way at the desirable goal of a total-space architecture, a hoped-for and a probable result of the current pressure toward sustainability. More specifically, a sustainable total-space architecture that goes beyond simple bioclimatic systems achieves just this through its efforts to internalize the externalities. It is architecture on both sides of the membrane and displays "creative fitting revealed in health," in McHarg's expression: an architecture at peace with the outside.

Ian McHarg pursued this goal. He tried to construct artifacts that had natural logic–"natural artifacts." He advocated planned habitation coherent with the characteristics of each biome, consonant with tropical rainforests, with deserts or grasslands or temperate woodlands. The biosphere is not at all uniform. From pole to pole, across the equator, inside caves and in the upland forests, exist a range of distinct situations, of climatic conditions within their corresponding extensive biomes. A fantastic diversity lies within the heart of each biome, today a striking consequence of profound change brought about by incessant human labor. The activities and plans called for in *Design with Nature* demand that we be conscious of the non-human diversity and to at least know its broadest painted strokes. Nature is far from uniform, nor can design be generalized. We need conceptual tools that help us recognize and thrive amidst global diversity.

These concerns brought me to conceive of *Biosfera* (in English as *Encyclopedia of the Biosphere*).[1] Ecology expertise is scarce and professionals versed in social ecology even rarer; this illustrates McHarg's "humpty-dumptyism," of course. Scientists, ecologists, or social ecologists provide specialized information in a fragmented manner that is usually inaccessible to the general public.

Even their professional colleagues take in, evaluate, and respond to the specialized knowledge in a fragmented manner. As McHarg insists:

> This is what modern science is; the egg is shattered, all the fragments lie scattered on the ground. The fragments are called geology and physics and chemistry and hydrology and soil science, plant ecology, animal ecology, molecular biology, and political science. There is no one who can put together again the entire system. Information fragmented is of no use to anybody. What we always need to proceed is really the one whole system.[2]

Not even the professional ecologists have complete vision of any region. Ecological and socio-ecological knowledge is fragmentary and barely comprehensible, whereas the cultural dimension of that knowledge is practically nonexistent. After nearly four decades of studying socio-ecological issues, we conclude that environmentalism is full of slogans and bereft of thought. There is much assertion and a lack of ability to act. Lovers of technology are ignorant of ecology and those who revere the natural often despise the constructed. That is, the realities of the bionomic complexity of the environment and of the importance of human modifications to that environment still have not entered our common cultural conception. *Biosfera* is a contribution to restore "humpty-dumpty." It is an eleven-volume encyclopedic work that reunites, structures, and categorizes the knowledge and the thinking of two hundred world experts with regard to the entire biosphere—the volume at the Earth's surface where life resides—and the incessant process of biospheric transformation by human activity. The experts on site or field directors of UNESCO Man and Biosphere (MAB) sites, described their reserves from personal experience. No citizen or ecologist has experienced all habitats—e.g., tropical forest, temperate woodland, ocean and seashore, island, cave, pole, tundra, desert, taiga, or marshland. Thus *Biosfera* is the only reliable and beautiful report of the Earth's surface as it is now. The biosphere encyclopedia is designed for everyone: teachers and students, literati, travelers, scientists, and explorers. As McHarg said: "Information fragmented is of no use to anybody." Most crucial is not how much we know of some one thing, but rather that we know enough about many things. Specialized knowledge by itself does no good to those entirely ignorant of it.

Notes

1  Ramon Folch, ed. *Encyclopedia of the Biosphere: Humans in the World's Ecosystems,* 11 volumes (Detroit: Gale Group, 2000).
2  Ian McHarg, "The Theory of Creative Fitting," in this volume, 33.

Part of a monitoring team inspecting a piece of forest duff.

# "To match people's needs with environmental opportunities."

An Oregon Forest: Local Knowledge for Community Design
Richard Hart

One evening in 1970, when I first opened Ian McHarg's *Design with Nature* and saw his layered maps of Staten Island, my life as a land-use designer took a dramatic turn. My studies of the sustainable practices in nearly millennium-old Christian monasteries coursed brightly about my mind. What I had found in the old ledgers and logs of those monasteries—the crisp descriptions in Latin aided by careful drawings—acquired a new language: McHarg's. His language expressed the vital geographical information that envelops location, whether neighborhood, city, or region. My pursuit that began then to find the tools and to hone new skills has not stopped. To design for sustainability is an intense social activity; it calls attention to the roots of all life with which we share space. I believe design of stable human communities is inherently spawned by one's sense of place.

In the decades since that McHargian epiphany I have kept a nearly constant focus on Nature's mantle, that part of the biosphere that supports, surrounds, and protects us. What have I learned, what do I use to maintain my focus? Like McHarg and his sympathetic legacy, I found that skilled observation is an effective mode to viewing through and between the strands of the complex weave of Nature's fabric. Identification of bedrock and hydrogeology, organisms, problems, and human desires—those features listed in McHarg's litany—followed by measurement and record-keeping are essential tools. Such tools are used to observe the region along ecological continua at ground level. We keep in mind another McHarg insight: what is the region?

First, one has to define the region in which one works. The region, in most cases, is defined by the client. The definition of the region is of course impossible, because the Earth is finally not divisible. So I say the region is defined by the person who defines the region. The region becomes the area within which the creative fitting must occur.[1]

The most satisfying path to sustainable design is the discipline of biophysical monitoring. When we study any ecosystem up close and over time, Nature reveals her condition: the directionality of the process McHarg identifies as "creative fitting revealed in health" versus its opposite, "reductive misfit revealed in pathology." Nature herself shows us where she is headed, her immediate needs and limitations, and how best to collaborate in her design. Her patterns, products of evolution, derive from her ancient personal history. They are never isolated phenomena, but rather dynamic and ever-changing; the patterns always form from sets of complementary constant and observable processes. Decade- or century-long environmental alterations result from the incursion and colonization by alien plant, animal, and microbial species. Additionally, shorter-term perturbations introduced by disturbance events lead to ecosystems in balance that operate through a ubiquitous property of the living: they incessantly exchange matter, energy, and information. Life forms interact creatively and, as McHarg points out, can optimally and creatively share one hundred percent of available resources and space.

The act of observing the layers of Nature's fabric–geology, soils, vegetation, creatures, climate, and history of use–requires one's boots to be on the ground, the very region under study. We mindfully notice that ground when Nature shows her best, in the northern and southern climes during her growing seasons of spring and summer. Change delights us with its observability then, when permitted by the mild ambience, temperatures, and light intensities we enjoy. With biophysical monitoring, we periodically step into Nature's regional landscapes to carefully measure and faithfully record what

happens at the same location over time. From below the soil's surface to the
canopy's top, each component of these landscapes supports the other, so
the condition of each is relevant. The soil (moisture, temperature, chemistry, degree of compaction, and disturbance), vegetation (percent of effective
ground cover, plant assemblages and associations), and the canopy above
(species, health of stem and bole, structure, age and size, rates of growth
and repair, inhabitants, and users) reveal the health status of the forest. Land
use over time manifests as roads and trails, fences and stone piles, foundations, waste dumps, and the rate at which they disappear into the landscape.
We now see the human activity, forest and wetland disturbance, the slashed
and burnt countryside from satellite and aerial imagery only imagined by
McHarg. These are recorded in the computerized Geographic Information
Systems (GIS) presaged by McHarg. GIS data permits comparison and analysis of human impact on local Nature. Traces of non-anthropogenic events,
so-called natural ones such as fires and storms, are visible from above: burnt
snags, broken and blown down trees, and stream channel changes. Yet most
of Nature's important health information is beneath the forest canopy, just as
most of our own health information is beneath our skin.

   In the tradition of McHarg, my students and I monitor restoration
attempts within a 267-square mile watershed on a national forest near Ash-
land, Oregon. We analyze and interpret many sources of data from the region:
hundreds of ten-acre permanent plots that we established. Our goal, to
determine the present health and future health trends of the watershed, has
been successful probably because we enjoy the work and find it relevant to
our interests. Although they seldom had it in mind when they first joined us,
most students choose to follow a career in the natural sciences. Many are later
offered scholarships because of the quality of their skilled work. Above all,
the bond to the land as they immerse themselves in and come to understand

Nature's web of relationships. So in contrast to the broad-based ecological approach of McHarg, my success in tracking of Nature's health derives from aid of the next generation: energetic and bright people, many between the ages of sixteen and twenty-two. Our "Nature's health" monitoring programs continued for four years often with the same group of students who stay with it from the ninth through the twelfth grades. Such community-funded monitoring projects should persist for at least six years; ours employs eight team members aged eighteen to twenty-three years old.

I choose academically strong team members with some experience in field work who wish to be trained and agree to work long summer hours. They are paid a wage comparable to that of members of wildland fire crews. They learn plant identification, tree stand examination, assessment of soil chemistry, condition, and chemistry, stream morphology, and aquatic life. They learn to map by use of global positioning system (GPS) receivers. Although each is taught the use of the total array of tools and methods, team members usually gravitate to the measurement of a specific set of indicators of interest. Often they prefer to work in pairs on the same plot and eagerly return the next season.

Our Forest Service monitoring work is driven by a vision, a set of goals that have been developed by the community and representatives from national environmental organizations. This partnership, a community effort, put together questions that define and inform the work. Its data and methods are available to the public via an Oregon website (http://www.lcri.org/monitoring). Results are entered into a relational database that includes active panoramic images of each plot and still photographs of the sample quadrants within them. Any number of site attributes and conditions, plant species or animals, can be queried. One can determine the optimal soil conditions within the watershed for the various ecosystem functions. As we work through successive years of monitoring, the watershed health trends that enable us to evaluate our restoration projects are discussed. We hope field data like ours will expand and be widely used by relevant environmental agencies that manage forests and other lands for planning.

Work like ours, we reckon, will aid other communities, their schools, and their students to participate in the stewardship of land in the public trust through monitoring. The best combination is a team that consists of enthusiastic and capable high school science teachers, willing natural resource managers, and a few dedicated students who want to explore the workings of Nature.

Such programs in the spirit of McHarg's passion, represent his "creative fitting"; these are absolutely required for any system, including social systems. Future generations of young people should be given opportunities to pursue careers while they help their natural home communities. Nature, in our regional program, shows her processes, her exuberant health, and her solutions to her inevitable problems.

Notes
1 Ian McHarg, "The Theory of Creative Fitting," in this volume, 28ff.

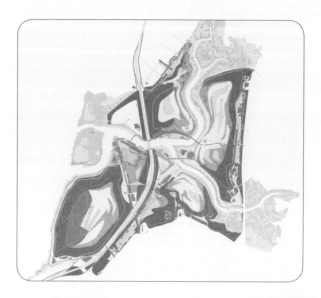

Fresh Kills Landfill to Landscape, Proposed Plan. James Corner Field
Operations has prepared a plan to convert 2,200 acres of landfill site on
Staten Island in New York into new public parkland. The project is called
"Lifescape," and is intended to prioritize ecological processes in the
reclamation of this otherwise sterile, hostile environment. "Lifescape"
is also invoked to imply new forms of cultural and public life in addition
to those of plants and animals, describing perhaps a more synthetic
ecosystem, where nature and culture can no longer be conceived as
separate entities.

# "Creativity permeates the evolution of matter and life."

The McHarg Event: An Unfinished Project

James Corner

Why are Ian McHarg's words so important for us today? What is said in the tapes transcribed in this collection that makes a reader sit up and pay attention? For some, especially those who share a proclivity toward environmentalism, the answer will lie in the clarity of McHarg's ecological message, delivered in a way both damning of anthropocentrism and in awe of nature and cosmic time. His humor, passion, and intelligence color already powerful rhetorical devices to make even the most disinterested reader pay attention. And his invocation of many different disciplines to form a collaborative and cross-disciplinary mode of understanding is both innovative and urgent, of interest to both academics and practitioners alike. University departments, as well as practicing collaboratives, such as Richard Hart's, can draw inspiration from McHarg's capacity to integrate specialized knowledge and to set up new models for interaction.

McHarg's exposition of ecology elevates that still young and emergent field to new heights of cross-disciplinary relevance. In drawing from concepts of environmental and organismal fitness—including thermodynamics, feedback cycles, creative adaptation and inter-relational systems—McHarg uses ecology to paint a vision of the world that is more complex, more integrated, and more based on dynamic interaction and levels of dependency than previous models, each limited in various ways by over-specialization and hermetic isolation. Indeed, his view of interdependency is so articulate that he is able to discern what is wrong with the concept of "environment" in the first place: that is, that to posit an "outside" in a dichotomously external environment is to distance that world from the inside, from us. Yet in actual fact we are inevitably and inextricably bound into the very substance and processes of nature. There is no environment external to us; rather, we humans are simply another specialized, unique, widely distributed and numerous part of a global more-than-human being. In this sense, human technologies, materials, and engineering works are simply amendments to and innovations of forms of matter "coming into life." And life, as consciousness throughout its history, now appears to be more than capable of not only perceiving and understanding its own place in the ever-evolving cosmos, but also participating, knowingly and intelligently, in its becoming.

It is this latter sentence that points to the urgent relevancy of McHarg's work. In marveling at ecological descriptions of the world, he wanted not only to seek further enriching modes of description but even more to move toward practice and intervention. As a landscape architect and urban planner, McHarg's primary focus was on the designed engineering of the planet for human settlement. He was not only an analyst and describer but an inventor, a maker, a practitioner who sought new forms and geometries to engineer a more wholesome and fitting world. An avid reader and writer of poetry, listener of music, and cognoscenti of art, McHarg also realized the capacity of perception, ideas, and imagination in shaping awareness of and sympathy with a larger human, if not cosmic, collective. In awe of science and knowledge, McHarg was also an artist, a creator, realizing that concepts are the primary tools with which we not only navigate but also project new space and reshape ourselves. In conceptually revising how planners and designers might view the physical world, McHarg also pointed to new sets of techniques and practices for action, practices that would reshape how people live, experience, and dwell in the world.

If the above points to a kind of larger McHargian project, such a project remains radically underdeveloped and incomplete. Too many followers of McHarg simply adopted a methodology for practice, and while most shared his ecological ethics and viewpoint, they failed to grasp the larger conceptual, innovative, and artistic dimensions of what still lies dormant in the potential of ecological concepts. This situation is further complicated by a general cultural conservatism with regard to the design of territories and space, more often leading to aesthetic blandness and environmental decline than to innovations or evolutionary products. Cultural habits and traditions are not, it seems, as fluid or adaptive to changing paradigms as many other processes and organisms which, while typically less entrenched and more fundamentally challenged than most cultural habits, will typically find infinitely wondrous arrays of new forms in which to propagate their history while projecting new potential. It is in this way that life bodies itself forth, evolving form, matter, and intelligence to new levels of complexity. McHarg opens a door into this highly animate world of actively evolving concepts, forms, agents, and materials. Who dares to step inside? And who can afford not to?

# Biographical Overview
## Ian Lennox McHarg (1920-2001)

November 20, 1920 Born in Clydebank, Scotland
Influenced by his working class Glasgow background and his
native countryside of the Firth Valley and Western Highlands

1934-1935 Editor's copy boy at Scottish newspapers. 1936
Withdrew from high school, apprenticed with D.A. Wintersgill,
landscape architecture, Glasgow. 1938 Enlisted in the British
Army (Clydesdale bombed in 1940). Served in World War II in the
British Parachute Brigade in Italy as a "parachute saboteur,"
participated in the invasion of Italy, south of France,
promoted to Captain, then Major, designed British military
cemetery in Athens. 1946-1950 Earned professional degrees
(Bachelor, Master of Landscape Architecture, Master of City
Planning) in landscape architecture and city planning from
Harvard University, Cambridge, Mass. 1949-1950 After his son
Alistair was born, he returned to Scotland. 1955 Helped create
the Department of Landscape Architecture University of
Pennsylvania. 1956 Son Malcolm born. 1959 Created "Man and
the Environment" course at the University of Pennsylvania,
Philadelphia, Pa. 1960-1961 Created Columbia Broadcasting
Systems series, *The House We Live In.* 1962 Co-founded the
landscape architecture firm of Wallace, McHarg, Roberts and
Todd. 1969 Authored *Design With Nature* / Originated the
theory of creative fitting (see pp. 21) / Defined creativity as
thermodynamic in nature, i.e. the use of matter and energy to
raise matter and energy to higher levels of order (see p. TK) /
Discerned that creativity always moves toward order,
complexity, diversity or dynamic equilibrium / Inferred that
evolution is a creative process / Described creativity with

the verb, "to fit," and pointed out its relevance to Darwinian fitness (of the organism to the environment) and Hendersonian fitness (of the environment to its inhabitants; (see pp. 25) / Undertook ecological planning as a process of finding the fittest environment for any consumer, helping the consumer adapt to that environment, while adapting the environment to the needs and desires of the consumer / Commissioned scientific studies from ten different subdisciplines as the basis for any ecological planning report, his "litany," (see page 28) / Built descriptive and predictive environmental and human ecological models / Along with Rachel Carson, Barry Commoner, Paul Ehrlich and Ralph Nader, popularized the "environmental movement" 1974 Wife Pauline Crena de Longh died / Helped 1500 landscape architecture Master's degree students, 150 professors, and 14 departmental chairs, and founded 20 new programs worldwide / Invented intellectual methods for development of "Geographic Information Systems (GIS), is arguably the single most important tool in urban planning / Originated the concept of Environmental Impact Studies 1977 Married Carol Smyser 1979 Resigned from the architecture firm of Wallace, McHarg, Roberts and Todd 1982 Son Ian born 1987 Son Andrew born / Consulted, taught and/or designed landscapes in Nigeria, Iran, Mexico, Taiwan, New Zealand, Australia, Japan, and many other places in Europe and the United States 1990 Received U.S. National Medal of Art 1992 Stopped smoking, alas, too late 1991–1993 Developed prototype database for the National Ecological Inventory with co-workers 2001 Died of lung disease in London Grove, Pennsylvania

# About the Authors

Ian L. McHarg (1920-2001) Born on the edge of industrial Glasgow during a depression, in a house that looked one way onto factories and the other onto farm and wilderness, Ian McHarg was from the beginning moved by the need for city planning to be integrated with nature. After serving in World War II, McHarg attended Harvard University, taking degrees in landscape architecture and city planning. He created the Department of Landscape Architecture at the University of Pennsylvania. In 1960, McHarg hosted his own show, *The House We Live In*, on the CBS television network, an early effort to publicize people and the problems of the environment. The show, along with a later PBS documentary, helped make McHarg a household name when he published his landmark book, *Design With Nature* (1969). In it, McHarg spelled out the need for urban planners to consider an environmentally conscious approach to land use and provided new methods for achieving it. Today Design With Nature is a seminal text in environmental architecture, and McHarg is arguably the most important landscape architect since Frederick Law Olmsted.

McHarg's method was to "begin with the bedrock" and chart each horizontal layer of the region from low to high: geology, hydrology, soil layers, ground cover, shrubs, trees, wildlife, social value, recreation, history, scenery, etc., by use of transparent map overlays. McHarg developed the mode of analysis today called Geographic Information Systems (GIS).

Professor McHarg's career influenced several generations of planners, landscape, and other architects. Beginning in 1959, his course "Man and Environment" introduced students to the complexities of ecological systems and the unique responsibilities bestowed upon designers for the well-being of the natural environment. Beyond his teaching, McHarg was a consistent contributor to progressive literature in the area of design, landscape, and ecology. In his autobiography, *A Quest for Life*, he outlines the influences that shaped his career as a professor and a design professional.

**Alan Berger**, an Associate Professor at Harvard University's Graduate School of Design, teaches courses in the department of landscape architecture. He founded and directs P-REX, the Harvard GSD Project for Reclamation Excellence, a multi-disciplinary research effort focusing on the design and reuse of post-mined landscapes. His book, *Reclaiming the American West* (Princeton Architectural Press, 2003) received the Research Award from the Environmental Design Research Association and Places Magazine, and was named a Colorado Book of the Year by the Center for the Book. His two recent books are *Nansha Coastal City: Landscape and Urbanism in the Pearl River Delta* (Harvard University Graduate School of Design, 2006) co-edited by Margaret Crawford and *Drosscape: Wasting Land in Urban America* (Princeton Architectural Press, 2006).

 **James Corner**, a professor and chair of landscape architecture at the University of Pennsylvania School of Design, is director of Field Operations in New York, author of *Taking Measures Across the American Landscape* (Yale, 1996), and editor of *Recovering Landscape* (Princeton Architectural Press, 1999).

 **Ramon Folch**, head of ERF (Estudi Ramon Folch) in Barcelona, Spain is also a professor at the University of Barcelona and UNESCO's Chair on Sustainable Development in La Plata, Argentina. He holds a Ph.D. in biology and specializes in socioecology. Folch created the Argentinian Pavilion at expo (Lisbon Portugal, 1998) devoted to Patagonian dinosaurs. He conceived and directed the publication of *Biosfera*, in English called, *Encyclopedia of the Biosphere* (Gale Group, 2000). This eleven-volume publication (more than two hundred authors) catalogs the history of the Earth's biosphere presented in context of the world's contemporary ecosystems. *Biosfera*, considered the most comprehensive and authoritative work on the state of life on Earth, has been translated from Catalan to English, German, and Japanese.

 **Richard Hart**, an ecologist who specializes in biophysical monitoring, works with communities that wish to sustain and enhance the natural environment that surrounds them. His initiatives include student and citizen participatory monitoring of restoration work in national forests and other public trust lands.

 **Brian Holt Hawthorne**, a Massachusetts state forest ecologist, lives with his family in the woods of western Massachusetts. He provides forest management development, planning, teaching, and research services to private individuals, nonprofits, and state and federal agencies. Brian studied linguistics and psychology at Wesleyan University and forest resources at the University of Massachusetts Amherst.

 **Adam MacConnell**, a graduate student at the University of Massachusetts-Amherst, is completing his Masters of Science degree in the Department of Geosciences. He was co-instructor in the Environmental Evolution course with Lynn Margulis from 2001 to 2004. He archived and curated the InterActive Lecture tapes (IAL) from 1998 to 2003. He digitized many of the IAL series to transform the original lecture from projection slides, reel-to-reel, and cassette tapes to a digital CD-rom format. The IAL program includes all audio and visual components of the "Environmental Evolution" series, including the Ian McHarg lectures.

**Lynn Margulis** is Distinguished University Professor in the Department of Geosciences at the University of Massachusetts-Amherst. She was elected to the National Academy of Sciences in 1983 and received from William J. Clinton the National Medal of Science in 2000. Her publications, which span a wide range of scientific topics, include original contributions to cell biology and microbial evolution. Best known for her theory of symbiogenesis, which challenges the "random mutation" tenet of neo-Darwinism. She asserts that variation in evolution is largely driven by the production of new genomes vias symbiotic association between different types of organisms. She contributed to James E. Lovelock's Gaia theory that the Earth with its living beings function as a physiological system.

She is the author of many articles and books. The most recent include *Symbiotic Planet: A New Look at Evolution* (Basic Books, 1998) and *Acquiring Genomes: Theory of the Origin of the Species* (Basic Books, 2002), co-written with Dorion Sagan. Over the past decades, Professor Margulis has co-written other books with Sagan, *What is Sex* (Simon & Schuster, 1997), *What is Life?* (University of California Press, 1995), *Mystery Dance: On The Evolution Of Human Sexuality* (Simon & Schuster, 1991), *Microcosmos: Four Billion Years Of Evolution From Our Microbial Ancestors* (University of California Press, 1986), and *Origins Of Sex: Three Billion Years Of Genetic Recombination* (Yale University Press, 1986).

 **David Orr**, a Paul Sears Distinguished Professor of Environmental Studies at Oberlin College, is the author of four books, the latest of which is *The Last Refuge* (Island Press, 2005).

**Dorion Sagan**, a freelance science writer, has published on evolution, cybersex, the biology of gender, and other topics for *The New York Times, Bioscience, Wired, The Smithsonian, Cabinet, Tricycle: The Buddhist Review,* and other magazines. His books include *Biospheres: Metamorphosis of Planet Earth* (McGraw-Hill, 1990), *Cooking with Jesus: From the Primal Brew to the Last Brunch* (BookSurge Publishing, 2001) and *Up From Dragons: The Evolution of Human Intelligence* co-authored with John R. Skoyles (McGraw-Hill, 2002).

With Lynn Margulis, he has published on microbiology and evolution, including *Garden of Microbial Delights* (3rd edition forthcoming, Chelsea Green Publishing Company). His newest work with a former head of research at NOAA, Eric D. Schneider, is a co-authored book *Into the Cool: Energy Flow, Thermodynamics, and Life* (University of Chicago Press, 2005).

# Index

# Illustration Credits